THE
MARRIAGE MIRACLE

BOB & CHERYL MOELLER

February 2010
From
Total Living Network

HARVEST HOUSE PUBLISHERS
EUGENE, OREGON

Published in association with Dennis Literary (Jan Dennis)

Cover design by e210 Design, Eagan, Minnesota

Cover photo © image100 Photography / Veer

Backcover author photo by Dan Stultz

The Marriage Miracle
Copyright © 2010 by MarriageVine Ministries
Published by Harvest House Publishers
Eugene, Oregon 97402
www.harvesthousepublishers.com

Library of Congress Cataloging-in-Publication Data

Moeller, Bob.
  The marriage miracle / Bob and Cheryl Moeller.
    p. cm.
  ISBN 978-0-7369-2710-9 (pbk.)
  1. Spouses—Religious life. 2. Marriage—Religious aspects—Christianity. 3. Compassion—Religious aspects—
Christianity. I. Moeller, Cheryl. II. Title.
  BV4596.M3M633 2010
  248.8'44—dc22

                                        2009035781

To Robby, Melissa and Stephen, Brent,
Andrew, Megan, and MacKenzie—
you are our sons and daughters, whom we love,
and with you we are well pleased.

Acknowledgments

Words cannot express how indebted we are to our dear friend, mentor, and colleague, Pastor John Regier, executive director of Caring for the Heart Ministries in Colorado Springs, Colorado (www.caringfortheheart.org). His decades of groundbreaking work in applying biblical principles and pastoral care to help couples care for one another's hearts provided much of the foundation for this book. For allowing us to generously quote from your many works and insights, we say thank you.

We also say thanks, John and Barb, for your willingness to be God's instruments in restoring and healing marriages for the last three decades. Thank you for your servant hearts to train others, including ourselves, to follow in this same ministry of caring that Jesus offers, "The Spirit of the Sovereign LORD is on me, because the LORD has anointed me to preach good news to the poor. He has sent me to bind up the brokenhearted" (Isaiah 61:1; Luke 4:14-19). As Paul wrote of his dear friend Philemon, we write of you, "Your love has given me great joy and encouragement, because you, brother, have refreshed the hearts of the saints" (v. 7).

We also wish to thank our friend Rick Pierce, founder of MarriageVine Ministries (www.marriagevine.com), who generously gave of his time, resources, and encouragement to make this book a reality. Thank you, Rick and Laura, for the numerous ways you have blessed our lives and continue to bless others through helping marriages remain consistently in the Vine of Jesus Christ.

We are also indebted to our friend Dr. Gary Chapman for his encouragement in launching our ministry, For Better, For Worse, For Keeps. His godly life, compassionate heart, and far-reaching impact are a powerful example to us all. We thank God for his extraordinary ministry that continues to bring healing and restoration to marriages throughout the world.

Finally, we offer our sincere thanks to Rod Morris, senior editor at Harvest House Publishers. Rod, you were the first person to ask us to write a book on marriage so many years ago. That first phone conversation was used of God to become a turning point in our lives. Now, almost two decades later, you were the one to encourage us to pursue this project. We can only say thank you for your long and faithful service, genuine expertise in editing, and abiding friendship.

Bob and Cheryl Moeller

Contents

CHAPTER 1

The Heart of the Matter

THE HEART of marriage is the heart.

That's why there's no problem, no heartache, no memory, no betrayal in marriage that two softened hearts cannot heal. When two partners choose to soften their hearts toward each other, it becomes only a matter of when, not if, the couple will reconcile.

Are we telling the truth? Yes, we've watched The Marriage Miracle soften hearts and bring marriages back from the dead.

Michael and Kaitlin were married only three years when their accumulated anger, hurtful remarks, and the outright contempt they felt for the other reached critical mass. Michael was exhausted and deeply wounded by Kaitlin's frequent and devastating tirades. After each painful and demeaning episode he was left with a wounded heart—a heart filled with a pain that was all too familiar from his childhood. Growing up he had often endured his mother's angry outbursts directed at both him and his father. Such intense pain overwhelmed his young heart, so whenever Kaitlin's verbal anger began shelling his heart, he would immediately shut down once again.

Self-Medicating a Hurting Heart

Michael was not without his share of responsibility for the deplorable state of their marriage. Starting in his teenage years, he had chosen to self-medicate his wounded heart with adult magazines and movies. Years later, with the advent of Internet pornography, he became truly in bondage. At the end of each on-line session he was left with a lingering sense of deep shame and detachment from his wife. Why did he continue despite the turmoil it created for him? At least for a moment, the explicit Internet sites made the pain in Michael's heart go away (that qualifies as an explanation, not an excuse for his behavior).

As is true for so many men, pornography became a powerful drug that served as a momentary emotional anesthetic. It temporarily numbed the pain of a lifelong wound in his heart. Yet because pornography always creates more pain than it relieves, it never resolved Michael's true desire to love and be loved. The good news is that when men address their heart issues and allow Christ to resolve their pain, the desire for pornography often dies a natural death.

Get Rid of My Spouse, Get Rid of My Pain?

With such intense and painful issues at work in both Michael and Kaitlin's heart, it's not difficult to understand how the day arrived when the two of them came to the same conclusion. They were each convinced that the other person was the cause of misery in their life, and therefore it was time to end their marriage. Their apparent logic (though in reality a deception) went something like this: *Since my spouse is the cause of all the pain in my heart, all I need to do is to get rid of my spouse and I get rid of the pain. Not only that, I'll be free to fall in love with someone else. I'll be happy at last.*

Michael and Kaitlin's friends got involved as well. For years the stories of Kaitlin's temper and Michael's addiction to porn sites were the stuff of hushed conversations. With the ill-advised encouragement of sympathetic friends on each side, Michael and Kaitlin's hearts became increasingly hardened toward each other. Meanwhile, the young hearts of Derek and

David, their twin sons, sank a little lower each time they overheard their parents' friends openly disparaging their mother or father.

The ensuing divorce was ugly (we've yet to see one that wasn't). To make matters worse, Derek and David were caught in the middle of the emotional and legal crossfire. Like most children of divorce, they would pay the biggest price for the breakup of their parents' marriage. Though hardly old enough to know all that was going on, their little hearts nonetheless told them something strange and awful was happening to their home. As the years would drag on, each would continue to feel the soul-searing pain of their parents' divorce.

An Unforeseen Plot Twist

Michael and Kaitlin's story would have ended pretty much the way most divorce stories end—with untold chapters of raw emotional wounds, page after page of the account of broken-hearted children growing up to become broken-hearted adults, and the epilogue composed of lives filled with lingering loss and a sense of waste.

Except in this case Michael and Kaitlin's story takes an unexpected twist, a plot turn so improbable that no one close to the estranged couple could have seen it coming.

Michael and Kaitlin decided to soften their hearts toward each other.

Kaitlin made the first move. After receiving personal counseling, she realized that the anger within was not caused by Michael. It had been smoldering in her heart long before she met him. She realized that growing up with an angry father had injured her once tender heart. The vicious verbal anger she directed at Michael was in large part due to the sins of the fathers being passed on to the children.

Michael had a similar moment of revelation. He came to see his addiction to pornography for what it was—a desperately self-destructive habit born of emotional pain and the strong deception of lust and sexual sin. As Michael started to address the hole in his heart he too had brought to his marriage, he realized for the first time that Kaitlin was not the problem in his life. It was the barriers he had constructed in his heart against women. Michael's mother, depressed and self-focused, had drained the life out of him as a young child. She had expected him, rather than her husband, to be the one who met all her emotional needs. Overwhelmed by crushing expectations he could not meet, Michael eventually shut down his heart toward all women—except those featured on the on-line sites. Now at last he understood why he was so attracted to the false intimacy pornography presented.

A Decision to Change Relationships Not Spouses

Kaitlin and Michael chose to seek help with the healing of their hearts. They went through a process where they allowed Jesus to disconnect the pain they had carried inside for decades. They went through an inventory of their lives and confessed their sins before a holy and merciful Savior. They chose to let Jesus rid their hearts of the bitterness they had held for decades. One by one they prayed to release the family members and spouse who had hurt them. The freedom they experienced in their hearts was almost immediate.

As the walls in their hearts began to come down, it became clear their marriage could be saved. After years of desperate unhappiness and loneliness, they realized a life-changing truth: *They didn't need to change spouses; they needed to change the relationship they had with their spouse.*

They had always assumed they needed to find a new spouse to experience freedom and peace. They discovered that it's possible to find true freedom and peace with the same person they married—if they were both willing to soften their hearts.

One of their first steps toward reconciliation was to confess their wrongdoings to each other and ask forgiveness. The writer of Proverbs tells us, "Fools mock at making amends for sin, but goodwill is found among the upright" (Proverbs 14:9). Kaitlin and Michael both knew that after years of mutually bad behavior, it was time for each to make things right with the other.

Kaitlin approached Michael with an apology for her years of acidic and destructive verbal behavior. She took responsibility for her ugly words and tone and asked him to release her from the moral debt she owed him. In return Michael admitted he had kept his heart from Kaitlin through his years of pornography addiction. Tearfully he told her his true desire was to connect with her heart for a lifetime.

The Happiest People on Earth—Their Children

Little by little each of their hearts continued to soften toward the other. Like children who first dip their toes in the lake to test the water temperature, they each began to cautiously engage the other in deeper and deeper levels of heart connection and communication.

After going through a process of forgiveness that unlocked their hearts toward God and each other, they began to seriously consider giving their marriage a second chance.

When they finally made public the astounding announcement they were getting remarried, the happiest people on earth were not Michael and Kaitlin, delighted as they were. It was their twin boys, Derek and David, now nine years old.

Friends and family fought back tears as well as they watched the miracle unfold before their eyes. Michael and Kaitlin were husband and wife again—this time deeply in love.

What type of miracle can bring about the resurrection of a marriage dead and gone for almost a decade? The answer is deceptively simple but incredibly profound: They both experienced the transformation of a softened heart—The Marriage Miracle.

Only a Matter of When, Not If, You Reconcile

The good news is that a similar softened heart is available to any couple today willing to seek it. There is no heartache, betrayal, hurt, or painful memory that two softened hearts cannot overcome. As we said earlier, once two people soften their hearts toward each other, it becomes only a matter of when, not if, they will reconcile. A softened heart can bring healing to any relationship, whether it's between parents and children, brothers and sisters, or friends and friends. Two

softened hearts will transform any relationship regardless of the problem, the past, or the people involved.

Not every married couple needs to reach the depth of despair and
separation Michael and Kaitlin experienced before they can experience The Marriage Miracle. A softened heart can improve the marriage
that has simply been feeling the stress of a growing distance between
husband and wife. It can bring relief to the gnawing disappointment a
couple feels as they constantly focus on each other's faults. It can even
stop the dead-end thinking that endlessly loops, *I married the wrong
person. I married the wrong person. I have to get out. I have to get out.*

Every Couple's Struggle

If you're struggling with a hardened heart in your marriage, you're
not alone. As descendants of Adam (and therefore heirs of the sin
nature) we all have the innate tendency to harden our hearts toward
the person we're married to. Though we don't get married intending
to harden our hearts, as our unresolved pain and sin begin to surface
(sometimes in as little as a few days after the wedding), we sadly turn
on the person intended to be closest to us on earth.

The truth is it's an ongoing struggle for every one of us to keep our
hearts from growing hard toward our spouse.

For most couples it's not a matter of their hearts being completely
softened or hardened. At any given time, our hearts are somewhere
along that spectrum that ranges from total acceptance to complete
rejection. What's even more important than where our hearts are today
is where they are headed.

When it comes to our hearts, direction is destiny.

We are rarely standing still in our marriages. Our hearts are either
moving in the direction of a softened and accepting heart or headed
down the track toward a hardened and rejecting heart.

We hope this book will help you determine the condition and direction of your heart. If you discover it's headed in the wrong direction,
we will try to help you find the road home again. Even if you have

lived with years, even decades, of isolation and loneliness because of a hardened heart, thank the Lord it's not too late. Whatever your marriage has been in the past, if you both soften your hearts, your future can be entirely different.

The Heart of All Problems Is in the Heart

Where do we begin the journey toward a softened and accepting heart? It starts by returning to the Architect, Creator, and Designer of the human heart—Jesus Christ.

The Bible tells us, "Through him all things were made; without him nothing was made that has been made" (John 1:3), and "For by him all things were created" (Colossians 1:16). The "all things" includes the human heart. At the dawn of creation Christ Himself fashioned the human heart to give and to receive love free and unfettered.

Jesus alone knows how our hearts were created to function and connect with one another. The capacity to give and receive love is perhaps the greatest of all gifts given to men and women (1 Corinthians 13:13). This is certainly true when He created marriage.

While Jesus discusses marriage in various places throughout the Gospels, He saves His longest and most important teaching on this topic for Matthew 19:1-12. In this remarkable exchange between Jesus and the religious leaders of His day, He reveals the underlying reason for every problem and difficulty that threatens a marriage. At the same time, He offers the prescription for healing every dilemma and quandary that can afflict a marriage relationship. While there is much more to say on this, we can begin with this simple observation: Jesus teaches that the heart of all marriage problems and their solutions resides in the heart.

The passage begins with Matthew telling us, "When Jesus had finished saying these things, he left Galilee and went into the region of Judea to the other side of the Jordan. Large crowds followed him, and he healed them there" (Matthew 19:1-2). It's important to remember that this discussion of marriage is set in the context of Jesus' healing ministry. Jesus was doing what He does so well—restoring broken lives, renewing hope, and performing miracles. In the middle of what was undoubtedly an atmosphere of joy and amazement, the opponents of Jesus suddenly show up.

It's clear they have prepared for this moment and even rehearsed their question, "Some Pharisees came to him to test him. They asked, 'Is it lawful for a man to divorce his wife for any and every reason?'" (v. 3). The question itself betrays their true motives. Rather than asking Jesus how as religious leaders they could bring healing and help to hurting and damaged marriages in their villages and towns, they instead want to know if divorce is permissible for "any and every reason."

Divorcing for Any and Every Reason

According to biblical scholars, the question the Pharisees asked was of more than academic or theological interest to them. They themselves were divorcing their wives for "any and every reason." Rather than defending the sacredness and permanence of marriage, they were actively involved in dismantling it. Their main objective in asking Jesus this question was to catch Him in an unguarded moment. If they could get Jesus to misspeak or stumble on the subject of divorce, they could publicly accuse Him of opposing the Law of Moses and use it to turn the people against Him.

But the Architect of marriage from the foundation of the world was about to set His own trap. He looks them in the eye and exposes their desperately hardened hearts with this penetrating statement:

> "Haven't you read," he replied, "that at the beginning the Creator 'made them male and female,' and said, 'For this reason a man will leave his father and mother and be united to his wife, and the two will become one flesh'? So they are no longer two, but one. Therefore what God has joined together, let man not separate."

You can only imagine how Jesus' detractors must have looked at one another in astonishment. They had come for the express purpose of catching Jesus in some technicality of the Law. Yet He had no interest in an argument over fine print. His heart was to turn them to the grand design and purpose of marriage as revealed in the opening pages of Scripture. While His opponents were hoping to find an easy way to justify getting rid of spouses to satisfy their own selfish desires, Jesus' focus was exactly the opposite. He explained that God never created men and women for divorce; He created them for a lifelong and unbreakable bond.

Smashing a Vase of Exquisite Value

We are often puzzled as to why people in our time, including many who say they are believers, are so interested in finding the loopholes in the marriage contract. I (Bob) have a television call-in show called "Marriage: For Better, For Worse," and I am often bombarded with questions such as, "Under what circumstances can a Christian get a divorce?" "Will God judge me if I divorce my wife and marry the woman I love?" "I'm thinking of leaving my husband. Is divorce the one sin God won't forgive?"

While there are legitimate and sincere reasons for asking such questions, in far too many cases we believe the callers have less worthy motives in mind. They are hoping against hope they can find a legitimate (biblical?) way to end their marriage, hook up with a new lover, and have God smile in approval on the whole thing. Such sad and undeserving motives seem to be driving the questions the Pharisees asked Jesus that day.

Why is this "how can I get out and keep heaven happy?" attitude so offensive to God? Perhaps a word picture will help explain.

Imagine you are a world-class artist, and out of deep love for a friend you give her for her birthday an exquisitely beautiful vase you had shaped and crafted. Many art critics consider this vase the crowning achievement of your career. They are in unanimous agreement this vase is a one of a kind treasure that could never be replicated or replaced.

Can you imagine your astonishment if your close friend, the recipient of your rare and valuable vase, approached you one day and asked,

"Under what conditions could I take your vase and smash it on the floor with your blessing?"

Just the question itself would likely leave you (and most others) at a loss for words.

How Important Is My Marriage to God?

Jesus was equally astonished that day when the Pharisees asked, "Can a man divorce his wife for any and every reason?" How important is marriage to the divine plan of God for His creation? Consider this: The story of human history begins with a marriage in the Garden of Eden (Genesis 2:21-24). It's a statement that marriage is the preeminent of all human relationships.

Furthermore, God could have used any means He desired to send His Son into the world. Yet He chose a loving and committed marriage as the vehicle for Christ's coming. While Joseph was only the human, not biological, father of Christ, it was through the marriage of Joseph and Mary that Christ was born into the world. Their relationship became the avenue God used to bring salvation to the world.

Later, as recorded in the Gospel of John (2:1-11), God chooses to invade human history once again. This time it is to inaugurate the saving ministry of Jesus Christ. So where does God choose for the Savior of the world to make His public debut? A wedding in Cana of Galilee. Is that just a coincidence? Or is there something about marriage that uniquely reveals the glory of Christ and His sacrificial and heartfelt love for us?

The wedding metaphor doesn't end there. The Bible tells us in the final pages of Revelation that history will end with a marriage—the wedding supper of the Lamb. It will be a grand and spectacular cosmic celebration that will occur after Christ returns in all His glory at the end of the age (Revelation 19:6-9).

The True or False Message Our Marriage Preaches

If couples whose hearts have hardened toward each other are to ever find joy, healing, and restoration in their marriages, they will have to recognize the primacy and permanency of God's plan for marriage. No other metaphor or analogy used in Scripture so vividly and powerfully conveys Jesus' love for His church. In Ephesians 5 Paul makes this amazing observation, "'For this reason a man will leave his father and mother and be united to his wife, and the two will become one flesh.' This is a profound mystery—but I am talking about Christ and the church" (5:31-32).

According to God's Word, the Creator designed marriage for reasons far more purposeful and mysterious than just so two people could find companionship, have their emotional needs met, or start a family. It was created to illustrate for the world the glorious, majestic, all-surpassing work of Christ. Marriage was created to serve as a living sermon that continually preaches the love of God manifested for us in the life and death and resurrection of His one and only Son.

That's why it's so important for Christians to live out in their marriage what a loving, intimate, and committed relationship looks like. It becomes a daily message we preach to a watching world that Christ loves you and me. When our marriages are harsh, unforgiving, and distant, we are perilously close to preaching false doctrine to the world. It would be similar to a pastor standing up on a Sunday and delivering this message: "Though the Bible appears to teach us differently, I believe Jesus loves His church only some of the time. He has a bad temper and can be cold and unloving. There are days He regrets loving His church in the first place."

Listeners would be shocked, and the church board would convene an emergency meeting. Charges of false doctrine and heresy would be leveled against the pastor, and rightly so. That same serious distortion of the truth occurs when Christian marriages display selfish, unloving, and mean-spirited behavior. Remember Paul said, "[Marriage] is a profound mystery—but I am talking about Christ and the church."

How we treat each other in our marriage is serious business to God. It's why the breakup of Christian marriages does such devastating and long-term damage. How many people have we Christians kept from pursuing a relationship with God because of our poor behavior in marriage? For many of us, it's a question we'd rather not think about.

Your Marriage Is the Creation of God

To summarize, Jesus refutes His accusers by reminding them in essence, "Marriage is a permanent, irreversible, and miraculous act of creation where the Creator takes two hearts and makes them one. Each marriage, including yours, is as much an act of creation as the divine formation of the oceans, mountains, or the deep blue heavens. Your question of how to reverse the irreversible violates God's very design and purpose for marriage. So why aren't you asking Me how to restore a failing marriage rather than end it?"

Despite Jesus' compelling and convicting answer, the Pharisees remain unconvinced. They are still looking for a way to justify the easy breakup of their marriages. "Why then," His opponents asked, "did Moses command that a man give his wife a certificate of divorce and send her away?"

The Pharisees no doubt smiled with perverse delight as they were now certain they had painted the Galilean into a corner. If He disagrees with Moses, He has for all intents and purposes denounced the Law of Moses. If that be the case, His opponents can justifiably bend over and pick up stones to end the life of this blasphemer. On the other hand, if Jesus chooses to say nothing, the people will recognize His obvious weakness and abandon Him. Either way they win, and Jesus loses.

At this critical moment Jesus utters for us the most profound words in all of Scripture that explain why marriages fail and how they can be healed: "Moses permitted you to divorce your wives because your hearts were hard. But it was not this way from the beginning."

The Root of All Your Marriage Problems

Jesus isn't saying divorce happens because someone commits adultery or because two people drift apart or because they can't quit arguing.

Those are merely the symptoms of the problem, not the real cause of divorce. Why do marriages end? *Marriages fail because one or both spouses harden their hearts.*

In every case we've ever witnessed where a marriage ends, at least one partner, if not both, first hardened their heart toward the other. Divorce enters the picture as the option of choice only after hearts have become callous, unfeeling, or even embittered.

The Marriage Cure that Will Work Every Time

"But it was not this way from the beginning," Jesus reminds us. A stubborn and hardened heart is never God's design for a husband and wife—it never has been and never will be. It is in this passage we find the basis for what we call The Marriage Miracle: *If two hardened hearts will destroy a marriage, then two softened hearts will heal a marriage.*

Stop and consider this question: Is there any hurt, disappointment, violation, abuse, broken promise, or betrayal in a marriage that two softened hearts ultimately cannot heal? As we observed earlier, when two people soften their hearts toward each other, it becomes only a matter of when, not if, the two spouses will reconcile.

Think back on your own experience in marriage or in other relationships. Perhaps you found yourself alienated or estranged from someone who used to be a close friend. One or both of your hearts had hardened toward the other. If that person is once again a close friend, isn't it because the two of you chose to soften your hearts toward each other?

We have heard caller after caller to our television program testify that their marriage was once all but dead and buried—until they both chose to soften their hearts toward each other. At that very hour a miracle occurred. A sense of renewed love, intimacy, and heart connection began to draw them irresistibly back to each other. Eventually, the two were reconciled and have enjoyed the best years of their married life together.

If each partner connects with their spouse's heart—maybe for the very first time in their marriage—there is no issue that cannot be resolved. *That's why our primary attitude toward divorce is that it's so unnecessary.* God has a plan that is so much better, and it doesn't require court costs, legal fees, or dividing up property. It may require a couple to do the hard work of seeking biblical counseling and other resources to restore their marriage, but once two hearts are softened, it's only a matter of time until reconciliation occurs.

Helping couples experience The Marriage Miracle—two softened hearts connecting for a lifetime—is at the heart of this book. In the chapters to follow we'll examine the signs and symptoms of a hardened heart, how hearts get damaged, the high price our marriages pay for living with hardened hearts, the steps to allowing Jesus to heal our pain and forgive our sins, the signs of a changed heart, and how to maintain a lifelong heart-to-heart connection.

Rediscovering a Childlike Heart

Before we bring this chapter to a close, we need to point out the remarkable postscript to the confrontation that took place in Matthew 19. Just after Jesus finished His encounter with the Pharisees, children arrive on the scene,

> Then little children were brought to Jesus for him to place his hands on them and pray for them. But the disciples rebuked those who brought them.
>
> Jesus said, "Let the little children come to me, and do not hinder them, for the kingdom of heaven belongs to such as these." When he had placed his hands on them, he went on from there (Matthew 19:13-14).

How does a chapter that starts with a debate over divorce end with little kids crowding around the feet of Jesus? Why does the Holy Spirit lead Matthew to put what appears to be two disconnected stories right next to each other?

The first story illustrates a hardened heart; the second a softened one.

Who will argue that the Pharisees had not hardened their hearts? Their cynical and conniving plan to find a reason to make divorce easy and marriage vows cheap reveals their true character. On the other hand, Jesus chooses to use little children as Exhibit A to show His disciples what a soft heart truly looks like. A chapter earlier He makes an unexpected if not astounding statement, "I tell you the truth, unless you change and become like little children, you will never enter the kingdom of heaven" (Matthew 18:3).

Why does the kingdom of heaven belong to people who resemble little children?

The answer comes into focus when we stop and think about the hearts of little children. Is there anything more trusting, forgiving, humble, caring, kind, believing, or innocent than the heart of a child?

We've raised six children together and have seen this touching reality firsthand. More than once we've needed to bend down to their eye level and confess, "Daddy needs to apologize. He should not have said what he did. Will you please forgive me?" We can testify to you that 100 percent of the time our little children would look at us and say, "Of course I forgive you, Daddy." They would hug us, smile big, and then run on to play. If that's not a soft heart, what is?

Can you see why Jesus says that unless we have a childlike (not childish) heart we will never come into a saving relationship with God? Doesn't it make sense that we can't enter into a loving marriage relationship unless we have a similar childlike heart?

Childlike hearts are softened hearts and will ultimately heal a marriage.

Keep the Focus on Your Own Heart Condition

It takes two childlike hearts to make a marriage work. One spouse's softened heart can often jumpstart the process of restoration; ultimately, however, it takes two hearts to bring it to completion.

What if only one of you is willing to soften your heart for now?

We'll address that issue later in the book, but for now we urge you to keep your focus on making certain your own heart is soft toward your spouse. The Bible never makes us responsible for the condition of our spouse's heart, just for the state of our own heart.

Can we know the true condition of our own heart? Yes, but it will require an honest heart exam, the goal of the next chapter.

> *Lord Jesus, You are the wonderful Architect and Creator of marriage. You designed the heart to be the heart of my marriage. Will You show me if I have begun to harden my heart toward my spouse? I give You permission today to start the work of restoring a childlike heart to my life and marriage. Let my heart be soft the way it was in the beginning. Amen.*

Questions for You and Your Spouse to Discuss

1. Do you agree that the heart of every relationship is ultimately the heart? How does the condition of your heart affect your day-to-day interaction with each other?

2. Why does a soft heart set the stage for the healing of conflicts in a marriage? Are there any problem(s) in your relationship that two softened hearts could not ultimately resolve?

3. What is the difference between a childlike and a childish heart? What is it about a child's heart that perhaps you wish you still had? How would your marriage change if you both had childlike hearts?

CHAPTER 2

How Our Hearts Turn Hard

LINDSAY WAS ONLY TEN YEARS OLD the day her heart was all but destroyed—
but her inner scars would alter the course of her life and eventual
marriage for decades.

Lindsay's parents were killed in an auto accident when she was just
a young girl. She was adopted by her aunt and uncle who also had
children of their own. Unfortunately, her aunt, Alice, suffered from
periodic bouts of rage, depression, and mood swings accompanied by
overwhelming fear and anxiety. Lindsay's uncle, Burton, was the polar
opposite of his wife. He was calm, disciplined, and reserved. He had
the ability to simply detach whenever emotional tensions in the marriage became too intense. He was the product of a home where even
as an only child, he was shown little emotional nurture or connection. To cope with such emotional neglect, he learned to simply turn
off his heart whenever its pain became too real.

The Coming Train Wreck

So the pattern was set. Whenever Alice felt rejected or ignored by
Burton, she would launch into a furious emotional attack on his character and person. In return, Burton would disassociate his heart (simply

emotionally unplug from the situation) and retreat into another part of the house until she finished her rant. When Alice would eventually calm down and return to her relatively right mind, the unspoken rule of the house was that everyone was to pretend as if nothing had happened. Alice's manic-depressive behavior was a family secret that was kept closely guarded.

This dysfunctional pattern set up the emotional train wreck that would eventually destroy a large portion of Lindsay's heart. The twin locomotives of her aunt's manic-depressive behavior and her uncle's disassociation-emotional detachment were bound for a head-on collision.

Call Your Uncle or Else

The train wreck that shut down Lindsay's heart finally happened one morning when she was in fifth grade.

Apparently Burton had said something early in the morning to set off Alice's familiar rage cycle. Alice followed him all the way out of the house to his car, screaming and cursing at him. He simply rolled up the car window and pulled out of the driveway. This left Alice in a frenzied state.

Inside, Lindsay and her cousins were innocently finishing their morning oatmeal before catching the bus to school. Alice suddenly burst through the kitchen door shouting, "It's time you know your uncle is a _____! I've had it with him. This is the last time I'm putting up with this _____." Lindsay and the others looked up, their eyes frozen with fear. Something in her aunt's face told Lindsay this outburst would be no ordinary episode.

Alice marched over to the telephone and nearly yanked the receiver off the wall. She spun around and thrust it out at Lindsay. "Here, you call your uncle right now! Tell him to get his _____ home and apologize, or I won't be here when you get home from school! I mean it! This time I'm leaving!"

"Uh…yes…. yes…Aunt…" Lindsay felt as if her heart were about to burst. She knew if she didn't get this right—and did just as her aunt demanded—Alice would leave home *and it would all be Lindsay's fault.*

Lindsay nervously dialed the number of her uncle's business and waited for someone to pick up. After what seemed an eternity, a calm female voice came on the line, "Hello, Johnson Insurance Agency. May I help you?"

"Uh, yeah, this is Lindsay Simpson," she said trying to fight back tears. "I need to speak to my uncle, Mr. Burton Simpson, right away. It's real important."

"You're his niece?"

"Yes...yes, ma'am, I am," she replied, her voice shaking.

"Well, sweetheart, is this important? I mean your uncle is very busy right now. He's with a client. Can I have him call you back later, say in an hour?"

"No, ma'am, I mean yes, ma'am, this is very important...it's an emergency. What I mean is...I need to speak to my uncle right away. Please, lady, it's real important." For just an instant Lindsay thought about dropping the phone and running out the door. But her escape route was blocked by her aunt who stood towered over her, her eyes brimming with rage.

"Well then, dear, I'll see if I can get him to step out of the meeting for a moment. Please hold."

Lindsay waited again for what seemed like hours on end. At last a familiar voice came on the line, "Hello, this is Burton Simpson."

"Uncle Burt, it's Lindsay. Aunt Alice told me I had to call you right away."

"Why honey, what's the matter?"

"Uncle Burt, Aunt Alice says you have to come home right now or she's leaving us! I think she means it this time. Please! Come home right away!"

There was a long pause on the other end of the line. "Lindsay, you know how your aunt can get upset at times. Don't worry about her leaving. You know she won't do that. You and the other kids just hurry on to school now. Everything will be fine."

Alice glared down at Lindsay. Lindsay's voice grew more desperate as she whispered, "No, Uncle Burt, please listen! You've got to come home! Please come home!"

Alice's face took on an even darker visage, "You tell that _____ if he doesn't come home I'm leaving for good. Tell him that right now!"

Lindsay repeated her last desperate appeal for her uncle to come home. But it was of no use.

"I've got to go back to my meeting now," Burton said in a near monotone. "You just go on to school and don't worry about a thing."

"Then…then…you're not coming home?" Lindsay said.

"No, I have important responsibilities here to attend to. I'll see you children this evening."

"But what if she leaves us?"

"Just do what I say and go on to school now, Lindsay."

Lindsay doesn't remember saying good-bye or hanging up the receiver. She only remembers turning slowly and catching the burning fury in her aunt's eyes. Lindsay's heart hurt so much she didn't know if she could take the next breath. This much she did know. *She had failed—failed at her only chance to save the family.*

A Child's Heart Withers

At that moment something inside Lindsay shut down—or to be more accurate, something was destroyed. That something was a large portion of her once tender, childlike heart. Years later, after she married, whenever Lindsay felt pressures of any type from her husband, she would do what she learned to do as a child—she would simply shut her heart down. Like her uncle, she mastered the art of emotionally detaching from any difficult situation and leaving it to others to sort out the pain and trouble.

It would take decades before Lindsay understood the true nature of her heart problem—why she had such difficulty feeling an emotional intimacy or connection with her husband or her children. It was only after a crisis that nearly ended her marriage that she sought out help from a caring pastor who understood how hearts can turn hard.

He said, "Lindsay, I believe your ten-year-old heart is still locked somewhere back in the kitchen of your girlhood home. We've got to go and find it if you're ever to connect with your husband or kids."

Reluctantly, Lindsay agreed. Though the pain and pressure that caused her heart to shut down was not her own doing, the bitterness and anger she developed in the years that followed was her choice. Along with the deep sadness, she carried inside a simmering rage, the common aftermath of childhood emotional abuse.

As she began to understand what had locked up her heart, she also began to experience the smallest flicker of hope. *If my problem is a locked heart, perhaps it can be unlocked,* she thought. The pastor gently explained how Jesus could disconnect the pain of her past and forgive her sinful choices that blocked her relationship with God and her husband.

A Crown of Thorns Changes Places

The pastor, Lindsay, and her husband spent an extended time in prayer together. He prayed that God would speak to her through His Word. He prayed that the Wonderful Counselor, Jesus Christ, would show Lindsay the true depth of His great love for her. "When Jesus speaks to our heart, it is always consistent with the truth of His Word, the Bible," the pastor said. "Anything inconsistent with the clear teaching of Scripture is not from God, and we must reject it."

With the help of this caring pastor and supportive husband, Lindsay began to pray through the experiences of her painful past. The pastor encouraged her to ask Jesus questions such as, "Where were You the day my aunt threatened to leave if I didn't do what she said?" As she did, she began to choke back the tears. "What did my aunt's rage and my uncle's passivity do to my ten-year-old heart that day?" she asked.

As she prayed, she discovered it was as if her heart were encircled by a crown of thorns—each barb sticking deeply into her once tender and childlike heart.

"Ask Jesus how He would heal a heart that is pierced with so many sorrows," the pastor encouraged.

She did so, and a moment later she looked up in astonishment. "Wait a moment, Jesus has taken my crown of thorns and…and put it on His own head."

The pastor paged through his Bible and read from Isaiah 53, "Surely he took up our infirmities and carried our sorrows…But he was pierced for our transgressions, he was crushed for our iniquities; the punishment that brought us peace was upon him, and by his wounds we are healed."

Lindsay broke down and wept as she had not wept in years. Her husband sensed that his wife's tears were tears not of despair but something else—tears of freedom. He reached over and gathered Lindsay into his arms. The two held each other so tightly it seemed they would never let go. For the first time in her 20 years of marriage Lindsay felt an intimate love and connection with her husband—and with God. The thought that Jesus wanted to carry her sorrows of the past overwhelmed her. Her heart was now filled with an overpowering sense of gratitude and love for her dear Friend, the Lord Jesus Christ.

There was much more work to be done in Lindsay's life, particularly in releasing the bitterness of the past. Yet she was on the road to a new heart—a softened heart—and an entirely new chapter in their marriage.

A Variety of Heart Disease

Not everyone enters marriage with a heart as badly damaged as Lindsay's. Thank heavens for everyone raised in a stable, secure, and nurturing home environment. Unfortunately for all the Lindsays of the world, the damage done from growing up in a painful home remains very real. It often impedes intimacy in marriage until the pain in the heart is healed and bitterness or other sins are confessed and forgiven by Christ.

Not all locked or hardened hearts manifest themselves as detachment or disassociation. John Regier, executive director of Caring for the Heart Ministries (www.caringfortheheart.com), explains in his groundbreaking work, *Twelve Locked Hearts,* the various forms a locked heart can take in marriage. (We'll explore these in greater detail toward the end of this chapter.)

For some it's manifested as a controlling heart, others as an abandoned heart, and still others as an immoral heart. Or it can result in a tendency toward a perfectionist heart. It can be a heart with a drive to accumulate things or a heart that erupts in anger and rage.

When an angry heart turns inward it can cause serious depression and lead to a self-focus. This hidden form of pride results in a near lack of concern about anyone but us. It neglects the daily emotional needs of our spouse and family. It's often very difficult all on our own to understand what's actually taking place in our hearts:

> The heart is deceitful above all things
> and beyond cure.
> Who can understand it?
>
> (Jeremiah 17:9)

When our hearts are deeply wounded, it is usually a small step to allowing sin to take root in our hearts as well. The psalmist Asaph shares his own experience:

> When my heart was grieved
> and my spirit embittered,
> I was senseless and ignorant;
> I was a brute beast before you.
>
> (Psalm 73:21-22)

We are born with a sinful nature. Solomon confesses quite frankly,

> Who can say, "I have kept my heart pure;
> I am clean and without sin"?
>
> (Proverbs 20:9)

Our sinful choices separate us from God, our spouse, and others in our lives. We come to marriage with heart problems already in place. Our hearts harden long before we say, "I do," even though many couples blame each other for their sorrows and hurts.

The Marriage Miracle attempts to show how Jesus Christ can bring healing to wounded hearts—hardened hearts—that have been damaged by emotional pain and sinful choices.

We Do What We Do for a Reason

While there is never an excuse for sinful behavior, there is often an explanation. It often has to do with heartbreaking and painful experiences in our past that the Enemy, the devil, uses to persuade us to turn our hearts away from God.

We were once doing a marriage conference on the East Coast in a church that met in a high-rise apartment building. Toward the end of the day a homeless man wandered into the back of the room. Several people from the church recognized him and nodded hello. He nodded back and sat down quietly to listen to our presentation about what locks a human heart.

At the end of the seminar the man came up and asked if he could speak with Bob. The ravages of years of alcoholism and living on the street were clearly etched into his wrinkled face. He said that he was divorced and all alone in life.

Bob quietly asked him, "When did you start drinking?"

"When I was nine years old," he said with sorrow in his eyes.

"What happened when you were nine?"

He looked down, took a deep breath, and said, "One day a taxi pulled up in front of our house. My mama, she just walked out the front door with a suitcase in her hand. She didn't even look back. No, she just got into the taxi and closed the door. Now, I know my daddy didn't treat her right, I know that. But she never told us she was leaving. She didn't even say good-bye to any of us. That was the last time me and my brothers would see her for the next 25 years. Yes sir, that's the year I started drinking."

People do things for a reason. Rarely do we get involved in self-destructive and ruinous lifestyles for the fun of it. Nor do two people come to a marriage with hardened hearts without a reason. Something has usually happened, often a combination of things that have locked up their hearts. In marriage relationships, locked or hardened hearts often follow a two-step process:

STAGE ONE OF A HARDENED HEART: UNWANTED PAIN

While the human heart can harden in a number of ways, let's focus on the two-step process we see happen so often in marriage relationships: *The first step toward a hardened heart is experiencing relational pain.*

As in Lindsay's case, intense and real emotional pain can cause us to shut down or lock up part (or even most) of our heart as a survival mechanism. Our hearts were not designed to be mistreated, abused, or crushed. God in His mercy may even have created us with the ability to shut down or isolate the emotional pain in our hearts. He did so in order for us to survive incredibly painful experiences. If we could not shut down, the intense pain surge might otherwise destroy all that's left of our hearts.

The Lights Go Out in South Beach

A true story that took place in southern Florida may help explain what we mean. It was a bright and sunny day several years ago when suddenly office lights went out, air conditioners clicked off, and elevators stopped between floors. A massive power failure engulfed the bottom half of the Sunshine State. Utility company personnel worked feverishly to find the cause. What they finally discovered was that a small fire had broken out in a utility substation. The moment fire was detected the substation immediately went off-line, setting off a chain-reaction as one substation after another in the southern Florida power grid went down. In a matter of minutes millions of residents were reduced to operating by candlelight or diesel generator.

The odd part of the story is how seemingly pleased the utility company spokesperson was. "The system worked exactly as it's designed," he boasted to reporters. "Whenever one part of the grid is seriously damaged, the other components are programmed to automatically shut down. That prevents major damage from occurring to the entire system."

It remains an open question if the customers of the utility were just as delighted that the system worked just as intended to produce a massive power failure.

This much is clear. The human heart was constructed to carry the life-giving high-voltage emotions of love, tenderness, and kindness. That's because they are made in the image of God. However, if the human heart experiences a sudden surge of emotional pain or trauma, it can often shut down. It likely does so to protect the rest of the heart from total and irreversible damage.

We describe this process when we speak of someone with a broken heart or a crushed spirit. The terms paint a word picture of a heart overloaded with pain or sorrow, too intense or too prolonged to bear.

Sorrow Overload

We all know of people who could not bear the pain of life. A dear friend of ours told us one of the saddest stories we have ever heard. It concerned one of her neighbors who lost his wife and all nine of his children in a tragic car-train collision.

In the aftermath of his unspeakable loss, the bereaved man for a year and a half simply sat in a chair and refused to look up or respond. His health deteriorated and eventually he passed away. "He died of a broken heart," she said, shaking her head in sorrow.

Our loving heavenly Father understands how fragile and vulnerable the human heart is. That's why Scripture tells us He sent us a Savior, who is the Friend of broken hearts. The prophet Isaiah, speaking of the future ministry of Jesus, said,

> "Here is my servant, whom I uphold,
>   my chosen one in whom I delight;
> I will put my Spirit on him
>   and he will bring justice to the nations...
> A bruised reed he will not break,
>   and a smoldering wick he will not snuff out."
>
> (Isaiah 42:1,3)

If your heart has been bruised and broken by the circumstances of life, you can take comfort in knowing how much God cares:

> The LORD is close to the brokenhearted
>   and saves those who are crushed in spirit.
>
> (Psalm 34:18)

STAGE TWO OF A HARDENED HEART: DISOBEDIENT CHOICES

While a damaged heart is not necessarily a sinful heart, it easily sets the stage for sin to enter the picture. That's why we believe: *The second step toward a hardened heart is making sinful choices.*

Remember the first phase in hardening our hearts is often the mistreatment or neglect we receive from others. But when we choose to openly disobey God's Word and His will, that responsibility is ours to bear and ours alone. The sin in my heart is never someone else's fault—and it certainly is never my spouse's fault. The Scriptures warn us that disobedience leads to a hardened heart:

> See to it, brothers, that none of you has a sinful, unbelieving heart that turns away from the living God. But encourage one another daily, as long as it is called Today, so that none of you may be hardened by sin's deceitfulness. We have come to share in Christ if we hold firmly till the end the confidence we had at first. As has just been said:
>   "Today, if you hear his voice,
>   do not harden your hearts
>   as you did in the rebellion."
>
> (Hebrews 3:12-15)

The Choice Is Ours

We all can determine how we respond to the hurts, disappointments, and pain that life (and our spouse) deals us. While we cannot control how our husband or wife might treat us, we can at all times control how we react to them. We can choose to love or hate them, to show irritation or exhibit patience, to inflict cruelty or offer kindness. All of these are our choices.

This ability to choose our reaction (with God's needed grace at work) helps explain why some people who have experienced horrendous pain and suffering still respond in forgiveness and grace. It also explains why others, when presented with the identical set of painful circumstances, choose to do the opposite. They deliberately take the road more traveled and exact their revenge while refusing God's grace. They end up on the dead-end highway of bitterness.

There's a true story of Allied POWs who were brutally treated by their captors during World War II. When they were at last liberated and their captors were lined up before them, one of the freed soldiers stepped forward and said, "There must be no revenge. There has been enough death and killing. It is time for forgiveness."

We know a couple, Lincoln and Hannah, whose marriage was rocked by adultery. Hannah, devastated by the revelation of her husband's unfaithfulness, nonetheless chose to respond with forgiveness and grace, and their marriage was saved.

Whenever someone chooses to soften rather than harden his or her heart in the face of deep inner hurt, we know God is at work.

Bringing Your Hurting Heart to Marriage

Many couples come to marriage with hearts that have been deeply wounded or nearly destroyed. Early in our marriage we opened our home to a teenage boy who needed escape from his abusive home environment. He told stories of how his uncle would get upset with his aunt over supper. To express his disappointment, the uncle would pick up his plate and throw it against the wall. The young boy's heart was wounded by living in such a cruel and angry home. He desperately longed for a home where the aunt and uncle loved and cared for each other.

When it comes to hard hearts, Jesus reminds us in Matthew 19:8, "But it was not this way from the beginning." God's original plan for marriage did not include two hardened hearts—whether revealed by plates thrown against the wall or by an aunt who threatens to leave her children to get back at her husband. Jesus never intended in the beginning, nor does He desire now, for two hearts to harden toward each other.

Paradise Lost for Our Hearts

What were hearts like in the beginning? The early chapters of Genesis give us a glimpse of a time in human history when there was no sin, meanness, bitterness, lust, rage, or indifference in the human heart. It paints a compelling picture of two people, Adam and Eve, who had remarkably tender and responsive hearts toward each other:

> Then the Lord God made a woman from the rib [or part] he
> had taken out of the man, and he brought her to the man.

The man said,
    "This is now bone of my bones
        and flesh of my flesh;
    she shall be called 'woman,'
    for she was taken out of man."

(Genesis 2:22-23)

This is the first recorded incident in the Scriptures of a genuine *heart attract*. God wired into the hearts of Adam and Eve a spontaneous delight and pleasure in simply being with each other. Adam's first words, "This is now..." may sound rather dry and unromantic. Yet the literal meaning of this specific Hebrew term is packed-full of intense feelings and romantic response. The response on Adam's part was joyful, almost ecstatic.

Then Bob Saw Cheryl's Face

It's a similar reaction to the first time Bob saw Cheryl. Cheryl was a first-year student, and Bob was in his second year at the seminary where they were studying. It was the beginning of the school year, so Bob was in the bookstore buying textbooks for the semester. Bob happened to look out the window into the hallway and spotted this incredibly beautiful blonde in a lime green suit walking down the hallway. Bob stood speechless, astonished by Cheryl's lovely face and form. Then a quiet inner voice whispered, "That's the woman you're going to marry."

Bob had never had such a thought before (at least not that many times). He introduced himself to Cheryl later that week and asked her to help out in a local outreach ministry.

Through the months, as their friendship grew into something more, Bob finally took Cheryl out to dinner. He told Cheryl in somewhat cautious terms about the first day he saw her and how amazing the whole experience was for him.

"So what did you think when you first saw me that day?" Bob asked eagerly.

"I don't even remember seeing you," Cheryl said.

Oh well, love is seldom symmetrical, at least at first.

Perhaps the reason Cheryl doesn't remember seeing Bob is that he was lost in the crowd. There were approximately 500 single men and 50 single women attending the seminary graduate school. Whenever a good-looking woman walked across the campus, she was immediately trailed by a pack of 10-20 hound dogs in hot pursuit (this was Kentucky after all). In the face of such overwhelming odds, Bob assumed at first he had little or no chance of getting Cheryl's attention.

Things might have stayed that way except for a fortuitous turn of events. One of Bob's floor mates in the dormitory knocked on his door and informed him that Cheryl and her current boyfriend would be breaking up at 5:30 on Friday afternoon. (Look, having good intelligence sources is a key part of winning any war.) Bob knew that Cheryl also happened to work on Saturday mornings at the receptionist's desk in the administration building, answering phones. His battle strategy was starting to come together.

The next morning, Bob just happened to be up at 6:00 a.m. He casually walked through the lobby of the Old Main where Cheryl was already at her post. As Bob remembers it, his suave and sophisticated approach immediately captured Cheryl's imagination and interest. As Cheryl remembers it, she just wondered, *Who gets up at dawn on Saturday just to get his mail?*

After a few minutes of playful verbal banter, Bob was ready for the pitch. "So Cheryl, would you like to go out to supper this evening with me?"

Cheryl looked up in utter surprise. The expression on her face said, "How did you know I was available?" To Bob's delight (and utter astonishment), Cheryl said, "Sure."

Waiter, Check Please

That evening Bob picked her up at 5:00 and they drove nearly 50 miles to a fine Southern hotel restaurant. There Bob treated her to a sumptuous seven-course meal complete with fried chicken, traditional spoon bread, and even shoofly pie. The evening was going just as Bob planned, until the waiter arrived with the check. Bob smiled at him with that big-spender kind of smirk and reached for his wallet...and reached again...and reached again. Bob tried to maintain a calm and sophisticated smile as he reached in every pocket he had.

"Is everything okay?" Cheryl asked.

Bob cleared his throat. "Cheryl, uh, did you happen to bring any money with you?"

"What, do you need help?"

"Uh, yes, I'm afraid I do."

Cheryl's eyes filled with astonishment, then switched to worry as she began to dig through her purse. All she could produce was a single dollar bill, and a minute or two later its twin. She also had a little change.

"Do you have any more money?" Bob said with desperation.

"I'm not sure. I mean, I don't know."

"Why don't you dump out your purse?" Bob suggested.

Cheryl looked at him and then turned her entire purse upside down and shook it. One by one, they began stacking pennies, dimes, and quarters in neat little piles on the table.

Just as Cheryl was convinced they were about to be shown the door (or perhaps the dish room), Bob broke out in a big grin. He calmly reached for his back pocket and produced the wallet.

"I was just kidding," he said with obvious amusement.

Bob can hear all you readers booing or shaking your heads in disgust. (Okay, he admits it wasn't a very nice thing to do.) Bob further hears you asking why Cheryl ever went out with him again, or as heaven only knows, why she decided to marry him.

The answer is obvious—our hearts were soft and our spirits tender toward each other in those early days. That's the way it was "from the beginning."

Rewind to the Beginning

We invite you to think back on the early days of your relationship before you married. Remember how much the two of you simply enjoyed walking down the street hand in hand? Or try and recall how often you laughed at his silly and pointless jokes? Or how much you enjoyed just looking into her eyes? How many nights you talked on the phone into the wee hours of the morning? That's the way it was "from the beginning."

Your hearts were naturally tender, pliable, and accepting. Perhaps it's because you had not yet caused each other pain or let sin determine your attitude. Your hearts were filled with loving acceptance and tenderness toward each other. If your beloved had faults, you chose to overlook them; if they had strengths, you chose to exaggerate them— particularly to your parents.

Yes, your hearts were soft and life was good. That's the way it was "from the beginning."

A Not-So-Secret Formula for Lifelong Intimacy

Hearts were soft and life was good for Adam and Eve. Following their first meeting and spontaneous heart attract, God explains to them His formula for a lifetime of connection and intimacy: "For this reason a man will leave his father and mother and be united to his wife, and they will become one flesh" (Genesis 2:24).

The Creator designed their hearts to work like magnets. Get the two anywhere close to each other and the attraction was irresistible. Their hearts were designed to form a bond that would be strong, unbreakable, and last a lifetime.

Living in the Aftermath of a Catastrophe

Unfortunately, we all live in the time of human history after the Fall of Adam and Eve. The day they rebelled against God, their hearts changed toward each other. Where they were once protective and drawn to one another in lifelong love, they were now damaged by pain and diseased by sin. They immediately began to blame each other and to attempt to cover their shame.

Their sinful choices proved catastrophic for the entire human race—and for marriages in particular. Now two human hearts, controlled by a sinful nature, repel each other just as easily as they once attracted. When hearts become locked with pain and sin, spouses can hurt each other beyond imagination.

Gabby was a beautiful woman in her early forties, married to Manuel, a hardworking and devoted husband. Together they had one son. Though she was adored by her husband, Gabby could not get past the hole in her heart created when her mother abandoned her when she was five. The result was increasing distance and detachment from Manuel and an emotionally hurting marriage.

The day came when Gabby was noticed by the leading partner in the law firm where she worked. Mistaking the adrenaline rush of infatuation for a true heart connection, Gabby and her supervisor quickly became entangled in a desperate and torrid adulterous affair. Gabby decided this is what she had been looking for her whole life. This man could make the pain go away. This man could help her feel truly loved. This man could fix everything in her heart. Manuel could not.

Manuel was stunned and heartbroken beyond words the day Gabby told him she was leaving. He tearfully begged her to reconsider, if only for the sake of their teenage son. He offered to make any changes in his life she wanted. He begged her for just one more chance to make her happy.

It was no use. The lure of the office affair and its opiate effect on her heart was too strong to resist. After living for so many years with deep sadness in her heart, she felt she could not miss this one opportunity to make it go away. She went ahead with the divorce and took her son with her.

You might be able to guess the rest of the story. It took only a few months for the great sadness to return. Only now, she had to carry the heavy guilt of destroying her husband's heart and shattering her son's emotional security.

Pain and sin can produce a hardened heart—and a heart once hardened is capable of doing almost anything. The hurts caused by hard hearts can run the gamut from merely disappointing behavior to the truly devastating.

Is There a Better Way to Heal the Heart?

Is there hope for Gabby and others who bring to marriage deep wounds and locked hearts?

That's the good news of this book. The healing power of Christ can forgive our sins and release us from our heart's inner pain. He can bring peace and freedom to the most hardened of hearts. When we invite Christ to soften our hearts, even if we have lived in an unhappy and loveless marriage for decades, it can be restored to the way it was "in the beginning."

A Dozen Ways to Harden Your Heart

As we mentioned earlier in this chapter, John Regier, an experienced pastor, gifted marriage counselor, and our personal friend, has spent much of his ministry observing the various shapes a hardened heart can take. He lists at least a dozen varieties: the abandoned heart, the rejected heart, the angry heart, the defiled heart, the detached heart, the judgmental heart, the bitter heart, the controlling heart, the self-focused heart, the rebellious heart, the immoral heart, and the temporal-values heart. We've adapted and paraphrased these categories from his excellent book, *Twelve Locked Hearts*.[1] Let's look at each of these in more detail and how they play out in a marriage relationship.

The Abandoned Heart. This damaged heart is typically caused by the loss of the emotional or physical presence of a parent(s) during a child's formative years. Whether caused by the parents' divorce, substance abuse, or chronic depression, the child experiences emotional abandonment. Later, when that person grows up and gets married, their abandoned heart still pulses with fear and mistrust. They struggle with nagging anxiety their spouse will one day abandon them too. As a result, they overreact in anger or paranoia to even the slightest difficulty with their spouse. Their negative response is triggered by the perception that their spouse is pulling away—a certain sign their spouse is going to abandon them.

The Rejected Heart. This heart problem is related to the pain of abandonment, but focuses more on a parent's lack of acceptance, love, or nurture. The lack of secure love for the child creates a sense of being unwanted or rejected.

Later in life, the rejected heart finds it extremely difficult to believe anyone truly accepts them, including their spouse. They constantly scan the horizon for new evidence that their partner finds them unacceptable, unworthy, or unlovable. That's why even the smallest of arguments quickly escalate into a full-scale confrontation. They feel immediate and intense rejection whenever conflict arises. Their reaction ranges from becoming defensive and combative to collapsing into complete despair and depression. This makes healthy conflict resolution nearly impossible for these couples. The honest dialogue and communication needed to resolve everyday issues in marriage is simply too risky for the rejected heart.

The Angry Heart. This heart condition is characterized by ongoing hostility, emotional outbursts, and simmering resentment. Typically, this person was raised in a home where at least one, if not both, parents struggled with hostility in their hearts. Anger, particularly for men, becomes a culturally acceptable emotional cover for underlying unresolved hurt and pain. In its milder form, the angry heart takes the form of ongoing sarcasm and subtle put-downs in the marriage. In its more severe form it leads to verbal and even physical abuse. The angry heart can never experience true emotional intimacy because the person's wall of hostility keeps their mate (and others) from getting too close. The result is a frustrating and lonely marriage for both partners.

The Defiled Heart. This is perhaps the most tragic heart condition of all because it's born of severe abuse. With one in four women experiencing some form of sexual abuse before age eighteen, it's little wonder that the defiled heart is such a problem in many marriages. It's characterized by a person feeling dirty, worthless, and overcome with self-hatred. The same tragic emotions occur in the hearts of those who experienced severe emotional, verbal, or physical abuse in life.

The end result is a distrust and fear of all intimate relationships. The defiled heart finds sexual intimacy in marriage threatening, if not altogether degrading. They are unable to respond in love, surrender, and trust to their partner.

The defiled heart continues to believe the subtle but powerful lie, "Something is wrong with me." The truth is the person who abused them is the one with the defiled heart.

The Detached Heart. This form of a hardened heart is characterized by an emotional shutdown or withdrawal whenever potentially emotionally painful situations arise. Known also as "the disassociating heart," this person has the ability to turn off all feelings of sympathy, empathy, or concern for their mate. They do this in order to protect their own well-being.

What causes a detached heart? It is often caused by such intense emotional pain early in life that the heart decides to shut down to survive. Later in marriage this is manifested by a lack of tenderness, availability, and response. This happens particularly whenever the detached heart is feeling threatened or is in pain. The detached heart is callous, unfeeling, and unloving and that usually produces discouragement and desperation in the spouse. All efforts to reach the detached heart usually hit a brick wall.

The Judgmental Heart. This hardened heart carries a consistently critical, legalistic, and negative evaluation of other people. It breeds a spirit of pride and arrogance that negates the possibility of true emotional and spiritual intimacy. A judgmental heart is often the result of experiencing early in life a deep-seated sense of inferiority or unworthiness. Usually one or both parents displayed critical and graceless attitudes rather than love and unconditional acceptance.

In marriage the judgmental heart sends this message to their partner: "I'm sorry to say this, but you always fall short of my standards and expectations." Instead of seeing their partners through the eyes of love and acceptance, they obsess on their spouse's minor faults, imperfections, and sins.

The Bitter Heart. This heart has made the decision to never forgive or let go of hurts and injustices. They believe this will form a protective wall, keeping them from experiencing further hurt and injustice. Paradoxically, underneath the layers of bitterness and resentment is a heart that was once unusually tender and sensitive. However, due to perceived and actual mistreatment, neglect, and abuse, the bitter heart becomes filled with unresolved anger and even a desire for revenge.

Regier believes the longer bitterness festers in the heart, the higher the price it exacts. Hurt becomes anger, then resentment, then depression, then despair, and finally it morphs into thoughts of suicide. The bitter heart cannot enjoy emotional intimacy because their anger prevents anyone from getting close enough to truly love and care for them.

The Controlling Heart. This hardened heart is driven to dominate or control to avoid being hurt or rejected. The controlling heart manipulates their spouse through fear, pressure, and aggressiveness to maintain a feeling of personal safety or security. In marriage this typically takes the form of demanding, directing, or having the final word in every situation. The controlling heart sees all conflict as a win/lose proposition—and they don't intend to lose. Such a fearful heart rarely experiences true intimacy because intimacy requires vulnerability, and vulnerability is an unacceptable risk. The true cost of a controlling heart in marriage is the loss of freedom, affection, and spontaneity in the relationship.

The Proud Heart (self-focused). This hardened heart takes the form of either outward arrogance or inward self-focus. Self is at the center of all relationships and decisions. While we tend to think of pride as a boastful or a self-exalting attitude, hidden pride can be even more difficult because a self-focused heart is always preoccupied with its own pain or needs.

A spouse who is depressed or anxious may become so self-focused that they have little or no energy to care for their mate's or children's needs. The result is an emotional distance that opens up in the marriage. The proud heart was often raised in a home environment where at least one parent was unable to get beyond their self-focus and offer the love, nurture, and care a child needs.

The Rebellious Heart. The rebellious heart cannot tolerate anyone telling them what to do or think. They push back at even the slightest request for compliance or accommodation. This is a difficult heart condition to live with in a marriage. It manifests itself in arguing, fighting, and refusing to cooperate even over small things. It is the result of growing up in a home with strict rules but little unconditional love or affirmation. As someone has said, "Rules without relationships produce rebellion."

The rebellious heart has trouble in relationships because of an inordinate fear of being controlled or mistreated again. They do the opposite of whatever they are asked to do. The rebellious heart cannot find peace with God or their spouse because they refuse to submit to anyone.

The Immoral Heart. This heart is hardened through indulging in sexual sin or immorality in its various forms. The resulting bondage often requires the person to give their best energies to pursuing false fantasies and obsessions rather than experiencing true emotional and spiritual intimacy in marriage. This hardened heart is becoming more common as Internet pornography and other forms of sexual immorality are promoted by our society.

Whether due to viewing pornography, a history of premarital or extramarital sexual behavior, or by fixating on fantasies and lust, the immoral heart is unable to experience true intimacy. The other spouse feels lonely, unattractive, and the object of their mate's lust rather than love. Often the spouse with an immoral heart grew up in a home where at least one parent struggled with sexual immorality.

The Temporal Values Heart. This heart is preoccupied with material, career, or financial success as a primary means of experiencing acceptance and value. Success and significance consist in the abundance of one's possessions or come from accomplishments or status. A spouse with a temporal values heart will often spend money excessively, work too many hours, or be preoccupied with appearances and status.

The end result is an inability to connect at a heart level with their spouse or children. They settle instead for the illusion that temporal values can bring them true acceptance and significance. As they put things above people, their marriage comes out the loser.

Your Father Is a Heart Surgeon

As we have seen, there are numerous ways a heart can grow defiant and brittle. Regardless of the form a hardened heart takes, it finds it very difficult to give or receive love, and the marriage struggles with frustration, loneliness, and a sense of being disconnected.

Fortunately, just as a human heart can be damaged and hardened, by God's grace and love it can be healed and softened again. Our heavenly Father is in the heart surgery business.

Before we consider the needed steps to move from a hardened heart to a softened heart, let's consider the impossibly wonderful promise of Ezekiel 36:26, "I will give you *a new heart* and put a new spirit in you; I will remove from you your heart of stone and give you *a heart of flesh.*"

Can it be true? Can God actually give us a new and tender heart to replace a locked and hardened one? Can that heart actually connect again (or for the first time) with our spouse, children, and others we value in life? The answer is yes, praise God, it is possible. How that miracle can occur in your marriage is the subject of the chapters that follow.

> *Lord Jesus, would You please show me how my heart has been damaged by my past painful experiences and sinful choices?*

I give You permission to show me the walls I've built in my heart that keep me from giving and receiving love. I want those walls to come down. I want my heart to be tender and accepting toward my spouse and others again. Thank You that You are the Friend and Healer of broken hearts.

Questions for You and Your Spouse to Discuss

1. What experiences in your early lives impacted your heart the most? Have you ever had the opportunity to discuss these with each other?

2. Looking at the variety of hard hearts, which one(s) might be true of you? Which one(s) might be true of your spouse? How does this concept explain the emotional issues that you have struggled with in your life?

3. If your heart were softened in these areas, how might that change your life? How might it affect your marriage for the better?

CHAPTER 3

The Value of a Heart Exam

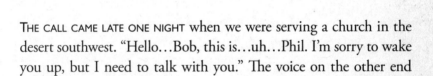

THE CALL CAME LATE ONE NIGHT when we were serving a church in the desert southwest. "Hello…Bob, this is…uh…Phil. I'm sorry to wake you up, but I need to talk with you." The voice on the other end sounded worried and upset.

"What's wrong?" I said as I rubbed my eyes and tried to catch a glimpse of the clock.

"Something bad happened at our house tonight. Something real bad."

I sat up and said, "Go ahead, I'm listening, Phil."

"I'm so ashamed to admit this, to say I did this. Holly and I were fighting and yelling, and I slapped her. I mean I can't believe I did it. I've never done anything like this before. We've had our fights before, but never anything this—"

"Is Holly okay?" I asked. "Where is she now?"

"She's at home…she's okay but pretty shaken. So am I. I'm calling you from my car in a parking lot, next to a supermarket. When I left home, she huddled in a room with the door locked. Pastor, I don't know what to do next."

Now I was wide awake. My first concern was, of course, for Holly's safety. Phil assured me that he had no intention of returning home that night. He knew he had crossed a line when he hit her. What he didn't know was where to turn. He was deeply distraught. His entire life was out of control, and he knew it.

We agreed he would not contact Holly again that evening. Instead, he would stay with a friend overnight until we could sort things out in my office in the morning. I warned him in no uncertain terms that Holly should have called the police, and if he made even a threat of further violence toward her, he would end up in jail. I would call the police myself if needed.

He said he understood the seriousness of the situation and agreed to the arrangement. I called Holly next, and after determining she was not in need of medical help, she expressed her desire to meet in my office the next morning.

Separation with the Goal of Reconciliation

Phil and Holly arrived separately and sat down in front of me. It was soon clear that neither of them had any idea how to resolve the crisis. All they knew was that their very survival as a couple was on the line. They lived in the desert southwest because of Phil's service in the U.S. Air Force, and they were a thousand miles from any of their extended family.

By the end of our first session, we all agreed that their problems ran so deep, went so far back in their lives, and had gone on for so long that no quick fix, sincere apology, or promise to never hit her again would suffice.

That's when I proposed something I rarely suggest—that the two of them separate for a season. I am not an advocate of separation for any and every reason. It's a serious step that requires thoughtful consideration, motivation, and planning. The ultimate goal has to be the reconciliation of the marriage, not its demise.

In this case, my foremost goal was to protect Holly from further physical harm. I made it clear to both that I was not recommending a divorce. Rather I was suggesting they live apart for a time for two reasons: First, it would give Holly needed safety and space; second, it would allow Phil time to reflect and work on his issues. The goal of the separation was not a trial divorce; the goal was to give each partner the time and space to rebuild a radically different marriage relationship.

Hearts Wounded So Long Ago

In the weeks that followed, Phil and Holly met twice a week in my office. It didn't take long to begin to understand that both of them carried in their hearts deep hurt from their pasts. Phil had been abandoned by his mother at a young age. He had led a lonely and difficult life as his father worked all day and was forced to put him in day care for nine hours a day.

Holly had wounds of her own. She had been deserted by her alcoholic father when he fell in love with another woman. Despite her father's promises to stay connected to her and her siblings, he broke those promises and the hearts of his children—particularly Holly's tender heart.

Neither Phil nor Holly knew what it was like to be raised in a stable, nurturing environment. They both entered their marriage with damaged hearts. Now the long-buried toxic emotions of anger, rage, and fear, coupled with the physical abuse that had erupted, threatened their future as a couple.

Was there hope for Phil and Holly's marriage? How could two hurting hearts overcome the recent violent episode and the weight of their painful childhood legacies? It would seem their hearts and marriage were damaged beyond repair.

You may not be able to relate to the severity of Phil and Holly's problems. That is good news. We hope your marriage is stable and fulfilling. Yet, just because you've never crossed the line into verbal or physical abuse, it doesn't mean that the insidious process of hardening your hearts isn't taking place.

Silent Heart Disease

Our hearts can harden so slowly, so imperceptibly, it may not be evident what's been going on until the day the bottom drops out.

We know of a pastor who was caught in an affair after twenty years of marriage. By all appearances his was a strong and stable marriage. He and his wife smiled at each other in public, their kids grew up, married, and started families of their own, and the church continued steady growth under his leadership.

Then came the stunning revelation he had been involved with a female parishioner for over a year. His explanation was that he had endured a lifetime of an emotionally dry and unfulfilling marriage. It was his wife's fault. While his words might serve as an explanation, they qualify as a poor excuse for infidelity. He had twenty years to address the intimacy deficit in his marriage. He chose not to, and instead betrayed his wife, children, and the congregation.

The process of hardening our hearts can be so gradual and undetectable that its most serious damage is often done long before we acknowledge it. Imagine if it were possible to go back in time and talk to this pastor and his wife at the twelve year mark into their marriage. Imagine if we could sit down and say in love, "Please, my brother, your heart is slowly hardening toward your wife. In another eight years you will meet another woman at your church, be drawn to her, and commit adultery and lose your entire ministry."

Perhaps he and his wife would dismiss us as nutcases or worse. "No way, Bob and Cheryl. We don't have any serious problems in our marriage. Sure, things are a little cool and distant at times, but we're both committed to the long haul. Besides, we both know adultery is the ultimate foolish choice. It's sin. It would destroy everyone and everything we've worked for. We know better than that."

Unfortunately, one by-product of hardening our heart is the ability to convince ourselves we don't have a problem. Denial and self-deception are fellow-travelers with hardness of heart. That's what allows the process to go unnoticed and untreated for years—we just don't wish to admit it exists.

We must stay current with the condition of our hearts. We dare not fool ourselves and pretend all is well if indeed it is not.

When Was Your Last Heart Exam?

How can we determine if our heart is hardening toward the person we married? We must periodically undergo a thorough heart exam, just as we do with our physical heart. Most medical experts agree that a yearly checkup is a good idea for people over forty. Some doctors even prescribe a heart scan. They know if you wait until you have chest pains and your left arm goes numb, it may be too late (50 percent of those who die from a heart attack never experience any previous symptoms). In the same way, it's vital we keep up to date with the true condition of our spiritual and emotional arteries. That's why the psalmist writes,

> Search me, O God, and know my heart;
> test me and know my anxious thoughts.
> See if there is any offensive way in me,
> and lead me in the way everlasting.
>
> (Psalm 139:23-24)

If anyone on earth learned the hard way that your heart can deceive you when you least expect it, it was David. His slowly hardening heart made it possible for him to eventually commit adultery with Bathsheba and then have her faithful husband murdered. David's spiritual heart attack nearly cost him his kingdom, his entire family, and his walk with God.

When confronted with his calloused heart (see the entire sad story in 2 Samuel 12:1-13), he repented and changed course. Unfortunately, the long-term damage was done to his legacy, and an innocent child died as a result of his actions. David is proof God can and will forgive our guilt, but He will not always spare us the lingering consequences of a hardened heart.

DIAGNOSING OUR TRUE HEART CONDITION

So how do we begin to diagnose our true heart condition? The process is simple though it isn't easy.

Step One: Ask Jesus to show you the true condition of your heart.

The Scriptures assure us God's Spirit is willing to help us discover the deep and hidden things in our lives. God is in the business of uncovering the secrets of the soul. Romans 8:26-27 promises us,

> In the same way, the Spirit helps us in our weakness. We do not know what we ought to pray for, but the Spirit himself intercedes for us with groans that words cannot express. And he who searches our hearts knows the mind of the Spirit, because the Spirit intercedes for the saints in accordance with God's will.

Imagine that—God searches our hearts and knows absolutely everything that's there. At first that can be an unsettling thought. Who wants God to see everything that's tucked away in the recesses of our hearts? Yet God's purpose in doing a heart examination is not to find fresh evidence to condemn us. No, it's so His Holy Spirit can pray for us in accordance with God's will.

Isn't that amazing? What deep love and concern our heavenly Father has for each of us even when our hearts are hard. He directs His Holy Spirit to plead for us before His throne before it's too late. If that's not encouraging truth, what is?

Like every other aspect of growth in the Christian life, a genuine heart exam requires our cooperation with God. As the old adage has it, "God doesn't steer a parked car." We have to be willing to respond to God's searching grace at work in our hearts with a sincere willingness to change and obey.

Before You Try This at Home

Let's be as practical as we can in getting a heart exam started. Consider praying the following prayer to express your humility and a willingness to obey God.

Caution: Before you try this prayer, realize it may be one of the most dangerous, life-altering, fasten-your-seat-belt prayers you will ever pray. Your entire life may be turned upside down and inside out before it's all over. There may even be days you momentarily regret you began this journey to know the truth of what's in your heart.

At the same time, when it's all over, you may well be more fully in love with your spouse and with Christ than you have been your entire life. Are you wondering just what kind of prayer can create potential chaos and exuberant joy all at the same time? Here it is:

> *Dear Lord, You have my permission to show me everything that's in my heart. You also have my permission to get rid of everything that doesn't belong there. Amen.*

That's all there is to it. Rather simple, isn't it? Yet it isn't a prayer to be uttered lightly. The moment you pray, God could begin right away to show you parts of your true heart condition.

You May Be Surprised

It's an amazing thing how God will speak to us if we are truly ready to listen. Once when I (Bob) was going through a spiritual desert experience, Cheryl gave me a book titled *Fresh Wind, Fresh Fire* by Jim Cymbala. At first I was too discouraged to even pick it up. Yet the day came when I opened its pages and soon found myself drawn to its powerful and simple message: God will answer us if we are willing to call on His name.

The power of that simple truth eventually led my heart to be pierced with the realization, "Bob, your real sin is a lack of faith."

I had no idea where that thought had come from, so I just dismissed it. Yet it came back a second time, now more powerfully than the first, "Your real sin is a lack of faith." Unable to shake the thought, I began to argue with God.

What? Me? A lack of faith? No way. I read my Bible every day. I prepare sermons weekly. I work in a gospel-believing urban church. I know I'm not perfect, but a lack of faith isn't at the top of the list.

Again the gentle voice could not be dissuaded. "Then why don't you pray more? If you had faith you would pray and lead your congregation to pray. You don't pray because you don't really believe in your heart that I will answer. You've tried everything else at your church but prayer, haven't you?"

I remember sitting frozen in my chair both afraid and drawn to what I was experiencing. As my heart began to melt under the presence of God, I had to fight back tears. Little by little I began to see the truth—my heart was plagued with a lack of faith. That was why I didn't call out to God in prayer more than I did. Was it that I didn't want to embarrass myself (or God) by praying prayers that I thought would never be answered? Or did I have too much pride to admit I needed help?

I came to agreement with God's Spirit that my lack of faith was the defining issue of my heart. It was the sin behind all the other sins in my life. That night I caught a rare glimpse into the true condition of my heart. It proved to be a turning point for me. The next Sunday I confessed my lack of faith before the entire congregation. I asked their forgiveness for not calling them to pray. I urged them to believe with me the amazing promise of Jeremiah 33:3, "Call to me and I will answer you and tell you great and unsearchable things you do not know."

What happened next was nothing less than a visitation from God. People poured from their pews and down the aisles at the end of the service. They knelt at the altar or dropped to their knees right where they were. It marked the beginning of a revival that eventually changed the spiritual landscape of our church.

Where did it all begin? It began with Jesus searching my heart and interceding for me in accordance with God's will.

He Wounds, But He Also Binds Up

What about you and your spouse? Will you give God's Spirit permission to search the deepest recesses of your hearts? Will you take the risk of hearing things from God you don't want to hear? Will you let the Spirit of God unmask and identify the issues that hinder your relationship with Him and your spouse?

Remember, God never uncovers things in our hearts so He can leave us feeling utterly alone and miserable. He brings these things to the light so we can experience genuine healing and freedom. Job 5:17-18 offers us these assuring words,

> "Blessed is the man God corrects;
>> so do not despise the discipline of the Almighty.
> For he wounds, but he also binds up;
>> he injures, but his hands also heal."

The process of softening our heart toward our spouse begins with asking God's Spirit to reveal to us our true heart condition.

Several self-assessment tools can help us hear God's voice in our lives. These personal inventories can show us the true issues locking up our heart. We will look at these simple and practical tools later in the chapter.

Step Two: Ask your spouse to lovingly share the things they see in your heart.

This next step in diagnosing our true heart condition is one that at first may seem risky or even foolish, but it will yield valuable and precious results. People are fallible, and only God's Spirit can see the whole truth in our hearts for what it is. Yet probably no one on earth knows you and your heart as well as your spouse does. Their insights have been shaped and sharpened by years of seeing you at your worst and at your best.

Again, a word of caution is in order. We recommend this step only for couples who are able to share the truth in love—rather than use it as a weapon. If there is a high level of tension or deep mistrust in your marriage, it's best to take this step only in the presence of a trained pastor or Christ-centered marriage counselor who can provide the boundaries that allow the two of you to speak the truth safely with each other.

With that said, there is great value in a spouse who loves you enough to caringly and honestly share the truth with you. As Scripture says,

> Wounds from a friend can be trusted,
>   but an enemy multiplies kisses.
>
> (Proverbs 27:6)

The apostle Paul also stresses the value of truth-speaking and truth-hearing from those who love us: "Therefore each of you must put off falsehood and speak truthfully to his neighbor, for we are all members of one body" (Ephesians 4:25).

Our friend Gary Chapman suggests approaching the question this way, "If there are two things I could change in my life that would make me an easier person to live with, what are those two things?" Chances are better than even that your spouse will know exactly what those two things are. The question is: Are you ready to hear them?

Again, this exercise is not intended to give you or your spouse permission to unload with both barrels. If you allow that to happen, it will only harden your hearts further. Instead, we must treat such invited honesty with great care. The goal is to build a deeper and more intimate marriage, not to prove a point or tear the other person apart. If you're not certain what will happen given the current climate of your marriage, it's best to wait. You can still follow the other steps encouraged in this chapter.

Lessons from the Refrigerator

So why take the risk of asking your spouse to be honest with you regarding your heart? Perhaps an analogy from the kitchen will help explain the value of this step.

One of the more unpleasant household chores is our semiannual cleaning underneath our refrigerator. Neither of us looks forward to this event. We pull the refrigerator out and take an honest look at what's there. We rarely like what we find. We have to get down on our hands and knees with a scrubbing pad, hot water, and a knife to scrape the ugly stuff away. Not much fun, but ultimately it produces a more sanitary kitchen.

The same choice lies before us in marriage. If we want to experience a genuine heart attract, we need to summon the courage to roll out the refrigerator. We need to give our spouse the opportunity to share with us the unpleasant things they encounter when they try to connect with our hearts. Though not without risk, it's a vital step toward softening our heart and gaining a new level of intimacy.

Who Is the Main Problem in the Marriage?

Phil and Holly, the couple we met at the beginning of the chapter, decided to take that risk. Though it was at times painful to hear, they shared with each other the walls they encountered as they tried to connect with the other person's heart. It took weeks of meeting together, but each desired to find out what was in their own hearts. As they did so, the road to healing and reconciliation opened up before them.

They both came to an interesting conclusion: *The main problem in my marriage is not the other person's heart, but my own.*

Phil put it best. "All my married life I thought the problem was Holly. I was convinced she was the one who needed to change. I believed she was the only person with the real problems in our marriage. I could not have been more wrong. I now see the problems were really in my own heart. It's made all the difference."

This leads us to the next step in doing a thorough heart exam. It involves answering questions that help us see the true condition of our heart.

Step Three: Take a spiritual inventory called the Personal Heart Exam.

The Personal Heart Exam is not a clinically tested instrument or a professional assessment tool. It was not developed by licensed counselors or marriage therapists in an academic setting. Such tried and tested tools are available if you wish to pursue those.

The Personal Heart Exam is a simple spiritual inventory composed of questions designed to help people better understand their heart issues. The first section examines the twelve different ways our hearts can be damaged (with thanks to John Regier's excellent book, *Twelve Locked Hearts*). The second section examines the thirteen sins that Jesus tells us come from a hardened heart,

> [Jesus] went on: "What comes out of a man is what makes him 'unclean.' For from within, *out of men's hearts,* come evil thoughts, sexual immorality, theft, murder, adultery, greed, malice, deceit, lewdness, envy, slander, arrogance and folly. All these evils come from inside and make a man 'unclean'" (Mark 7:20-23).

The Personal Heart Examination and Scoring Key are available in the back of the book (see Appendix 5). You should take the Personal Heart Exam separately from your spouse. You may reach a point where the two of you wish to sit down together with a pastor or Christian counselor and examine the results. For now, the important thing is to discover where your own heart damage and heart sins may be contributing to the difficulties in your marriage. If God is to soften your hearts, you must first know and acknowledge the nature of your heart problems.

The Scoring Key is quite simple and can help identify which heart issues are at work in your life. For example, the more often you check bitterness as an issue, the more likely it is that an attitude of unforgiveness is blocking your heart. The more often you check statements that point to greed or malice in your life, the more likely these problems are hindering your marriage as well. The goal is to gain an awareness of the areas where you have hardened your heart.

Once we know what issues are locking our hearts, we can come to Jesus in prayer and ask Him to disconnect the pain and forgive the sin. We will examine how we do that in later chapters.

Step Four. Take a simple self-test called The Emotional Pain Words Worksheet.

The fourth step in diagnosing our true heart condition is to look at the pain we feel in our hearts day after day. Though we know it's there, we may have never stopped and analyzed what types of pain we are experiencing. There is great value in actually putting words to what we are feeling.

The Emotional Pain Words worksheet was developed by John Regier and has been used with hundreds and hundreds of couples. (See Appendix 4. We encourage you to make two photocopies of the worksheet, one for each of you.) This worksheet will help you discover the emotional pain at work in your life and marriage. This worksheet is also not a scientifically tested tool. Rather it's intended to help clarify what damaging emotions are at work in you.

The worksheet lists two hundred different emotional pain words we can experience in life. (Isn't it sad that in this fallen world we can experience heart sorrow and anguish in hundreds of ways?) The worksheet will help you identify the major emotional pain issues that have likely caused you to shut down your heart. Circle the words that best describe the pain you feel, and beside each word you circle, write a number from one to ten. One indicates a low-level intensity of pain while ten indicates the highest level. Then review the words you circled paying the most attention to the words with the higher numbers next to them. Those likely are the pains that are locking your heart.

To find healing and victory over these painful emotions, you must first be aware of what they are.

Am I a Mistake?

A woman was once told by her mother that she had hoped to give birth to a boy instead. As a result, the young girl grew up believing she was a mistake. If she took the Emotional Pain Words worksheet, she would likely circle words such as *unwanted* and *rejected* and *mistake*. A strong sense of rejection made it difficult for her to give and receive love in marriage; it locked her heart toward her husband. She was convinced she was a mistake, and no one can love a mistake (or so she thought).

To find true heart healing she would need to challenge a lifetime of negative thoughts and replace them with positive biblical truths. She could turn to God's promises, such as Ephesians 2:10, "For we are God's workmanship, created in Christ Jesus to do good works, which God prepared in advance for us to do."

If she did so, she would over time come to believe the truth that God wanted a girl, not a boy, when she was born. Her gender was part of His plan for her life before the creation of the world. When we understand the specific pain at work in our lives, God's Word can bring healing. Jesus promises in John 8:32, "Then you will know the truth, and the truth will set you free."

Step Five: Make a list of how other people, your family, and your spouse have hurt you.

Once we have identified the pain that lingers in our hearts, there is value in going back to discover who and what caused it. Only then can we begin to find freedom and release. This brings us to the fifth step in diagnosing our true heart condition: writing down the names of the significant people who affected our life in a negative and painful way.

The purpose of this exercise is not to encourage a victim mentality. Heaven forbid, for the Bible encourages us to have a victorious mentality, "And we know that in all things God works for the good of those who love him, who have been called according to his purpose... No, in all these things we are more than conquerors through him who loved us" (Romans 8:28,37). God's Word teaches we are to deal with past pain from the perspective of a victor not a victim.

At the same time, the Bible calls us to take responsibility for our lives, to forgive others, and to admit the choices we've made in response to the hurts and pain others have caused us. To do this we need to list one by one how other people have hurt us significantly, including our family and our spouse. Only then can we begin the needed work of forgiving each person. This involves us releasing them from the moral debt they owe us. It's not necessary to recall each person on earth who has ever slighted or offended you. Rather, focus on those people whose actions left an enduring painful mark on your life.

(Appendixes 1-3 include three worksheets—My Spouse Who Has Hurt Me, Family Members Who Have Hurt Me, and People Who Have Hurt Me—to facilitate this process.)

Has the Pain Been Buried Alive?

Facing the past may be a difficult, even traumatic, experience. It may dredge up old memories and experiences you prefer to leave buried. Yet, unhealed wounds when buried are buried alive. The purpose of this exercise is to understand what painful memories and experiences may still be controlling you and blocking intimacy in your marriage. It can make all the difference in the process of softening your heart.

Even the great apostle Paul acknowledged the names of those who had caused him great hurt and grief. In 2 Timothy 4:14 he writes, "Alexander the metalworker did me a great deal of harm. The Lord will repay him for what he has done. You too should be on your guard against him, because he strongly opposed our message."

There is redemptive value in honestly identifying those people who have caused us harm—that is, if we then follow through with Paul's command in Colossians 3:13, "Bear with each other and forgive each other whatever grievances you have against one another. Forgive as the Lord forgave you."

We will save our discussion of the specific forgiveness process for a later chapter. However, we believe it is beneficial now to lay the groundwork for understanding why forgiving those who have hurt us is so important in softening our hearts toward our spouse.

The Day the World Stood Still

We learned in earlier chapters that a hardened heart is a heart with walls. Those walls prevent a person from giving and receiving love. Bitterness and unforgiveness are often the primary bricks that lock up a heart. Even if we are resentful toward someone other than our spouse, that bitterness spills over and hinders our ability to love our husband or wife.

When we face our bitterness and get rid of it, the wall in our heart starts to come down, and we make an amazing discovery—it's not the person we forgive who goes free; it's ourselves. We no longer have to live with a blockade in our heart constructed of anger, resentment, or bitterness toward the offender. We are now free to give love and receive love—something that harboring unforgiveness never allowed us to do.

Consider the true story of what happened years ago in Niagara Falls, New York. One March morning the residents of the famous honeymoon village woke up to the sound of something they had never heard before—complete silence. Astonished villagers filed into the streets in disbelief—the mighty Niagara Falls had stopped. It was bone dry. Some terrified residents concluded the end of the world had arrived and their doom was imminent.

The truth of the matter proved to be far less apocalyptic. An early spring thaw on the Great Lakes had sent gigantic ice chunks floating down the mouth of the Niagara River. In a rare coincidence of nature, the mammoth ice floes locked together and formed an impenetrable ice dam. The wall of ice choked off all water leading to Niagara Falls.

This freak of nature lasted for almost forty-eight hours. Then the shifting currents and the wind and the warmth of the sun caused the ice dam to break up. As soon as it gave way, millions of gallons cascaded down the river, and soon the world's most famous waterfall was back in business.

Is Your Heart a River or a Dam?

The story gives us a marvelous word picture of what happens in our hearts when we don't forgive those who have hurt us. The accumulated years of bitterness, resentment, and frustration coalesce to form ice jams that choke off the flow of love and intimacy in our hearts. The frozen wall of bitterness blocks all attempts to form close and satisfying relationships with those we love. Once we forgive those who have hurt us and release them from the moral debt they owe us, the current of love and intimacy rushes through our hearts once again, creating a marriage with amazing attraction and connection.

Writing down the names of those who have hurt us is not for the purpose of locating culprits from our past so we can punish them. Instead, it's so we can offer them the forgiveness they need and experience the heart-release we so desperately need. The end result is a steady stream of love flowing from our hearts to our spouse and those we love most.

If we are to soften our hearts toward our spouse, we must begin by allowing God to do a genuine heart exam.

Phil and Holly, the couple we met at the beginning of this chapter, went through such a process. They forgave one by one those who had done so much to damage their hearts. They released them from the moral debts they owed them. As God began to soften Phil and Holly's hearts, the walls came down. Eventually the day arrived when their hearts were connected. With their positive problem-solving skills now in place, it was safe for them to live together as a couple once again.

Their marriage, like most of ours, is a work in progress. True heart intimacy will always be a journey not a destination. However, if you were to ask them what's changed in their marriage, they would likely say that, rather than attacking each other, they now reach out to each other's heart. You can see the result of their softened hearts on their smiling faces.

Are you willing to let God do the same kind of miracle in your marriage? It begins by praying David's prayer in Psalm 139:23-24,

> Search me, O God, and know my heart;
>   test me and know my anxious thoughts.
> See if there is any offensive way in me,
>   and lead me in the way everlasting.

The Power to Soften Your Hearts

People often ask, "Where can I find the strength or desire to soften my heart toward my spouse? We have such a difficult and painful relationship history. I just don't know if I can trust again, forgive, and let go of the past. So how do I find the strength to start over?"

That's an important question, and one we'll answer with an analogy.

Imagine the two of you set up a new home in a cabin on the Colorado River next to the great Hoover Dam. However, when it comes to providing electricity for your home, you choose to use only a small gas generator in back of the cabin. At best, it gives you a few hours of electricity each day. The rest of the time you get by using candlelight or an occasional flashlight.

What a shame to spend so many hours in the dark when right next to you is an inexhaustible source of energy. If you tapped into that energy source, it could provide millions of kilowatts of power each day and never run out.

It's that way when it comes to building a marriage. We can either try to build a marriage on the limited amount of love, acceptance, and forgiveness we have in our own hearts. Or we can establish our marriage by tapping into the limitless supply of love, acceptance, and forgiveness found in the heart of God.

Which makes the most sense?

Steps to a Life-Changing Connection with God

For those of you wishing to tap into the exhaustible supply of God's love to power your marriage relationship, let me suggest you do the following:

1. Confess (agree) with God that you are a sinner and have fallen short of His glorious standard.

We begin the journey to a new relationship with God by admitting that our sin and hard hearts have created a barrier. It stands as a wall between God and our own hearts. Romans 3:23-24 tells us, "There is no difference, for all have sinned and fall short of the glory of God, and are justified freely by his grace through the redemption that came by Christ Jesus." To take down this wall, the Bible tells us we have to confess or agree with God that our sins have separated us from Him and each other.

Many individuals find the idea of confession undesirable or unnecessary. They argue that they are just as good as anyone else and certainly no worse. Why should they label themselves as a sinner?

The truth is that just one sin is enough to separate us from an eternal relationship with God. The first step toward reconciliation and a new start is to confess our sins.

2. Repent (change your mind) and ask God to forgive you based on the finished work of Jesus Christ on the cross for us.

The next step to entering into a new relationship with God is to change our minds. Whereas we once believed we didn't need Christ in our hearts to live life or build a marriage, we now see that we were wrong. The Bible says, "Repent, then, and turn to God, so that your sins may be wiped out, that times of refreshing may come from the Lord" (Acts 3:19).

Again, many people don't see the problem with letting God run part of their lives but reserving control of the rest for themselves. They don't see allowing a sin here or there to make that much of a difference.

To receive Jesus Christ into our hearts, we have to admit that regardless of how many good works and good motives we have, the wrong actions and bad motives will ultimately ruin the whole mix. Repentance is changing our mind and asking God to forgive and remove our sins, rather than trying to excuse or justify them.

3. Believe (put your trust in Christ alone) for the promise of salvation.

Perhaps the most important question in life is, "Who or what am I ultimately trusting in for my eternal destiny?" Some people are trusting in their good character or good works. Some are trusting in the god they believe is within each person. Yet others are trusting in the idea that all roads lead to God, therefore it really doesn't matter which one you take.

The Scriptures tell us, "Yet to all who received him, to those who believed in his name [the name of Jesus Christ], he gave the right to become children of God" (John 1:12).

Many of us use a global positioning system (GPS) so we can find the fastest and most direct route to our destination. Imagine if we were to turn ours on one day and the soothing voice with an English accent said, "I know you want to drive to Colorado Springs from Denver. Take any road you like. Go north or south or east or west. It really doesn't matter. All roads in the world lead to Colorado Springs. Let's be reasonable. It may be that the road that works for you may not work for another person. So just choose the road that you really believe in, and it will get you there."

No matter how much we sincerely believed that by going north from Denver we would eventually reach Colorado Springs, the truth is we would be headed to Montana or Wyoming, not the Springs.

It's that way with spiritual truth. All roads do not lead to God; in fact, all but one leads us in the wrong direction. Only the road that takes us to the finished work of Jesus Christ will lead us ultimately to God and eternal life. That's not my opinion, that's the teaching of God's Word, "Salvation is found in no one else, for there is no other name under heaven given to men by which we must be saved" (Acts 4:12).

For the two of you to make a new start to your marriage and soften your hearts, you must turn to the one and only way God has opened for us to find forgiveness of sin and eternal life. The final words of Jesus when He died upon the cross were, "It is finished." That means He paid the entire penalty for your sins and mine. By placing our trust in that sacrifice, we can be finished with all the things that once created barriers in our hearts between us and God and between us and each other.

4. Receive (accept God's offer) of grace and the gift of eternal life.

This truly is a gift from God, as the Bible explains, "For it is by grace you have been saved, through faith—and this not from your-selves, it is the gift of God—not by works, so that no one can boast" (Ephesians 2:8-9). One of the most difficult things to get our arms around is that we can do nothing to earn or deserve the forgiveness of our sins. It's our human nature (perhaps because of pride) to insist that we must do something to earn our way into heaven.

The fact remains that heaven is a free gift. It was purchased at great price by the death of Jesus Christ. God takes great delight in being able to make this amazing offer to us. It's similar to the pleasure we received when we gave our future wife her engagement ring. Imagine if that event had gone something like this.

You spend days, even weeks shopping for exactly the right diamond. When you find it, you realize it will cost you your entire life's savings. No matter. You are so in love, you withdraw the entire amount and purchase the ring.

Then, after a very special dinner, you present her with the box. She opens it and her eyes light up in amazement. She is at a loss for words as she tries on the ring. When at last she can speak, she says, "Oh thank you, Sweetheart. It's absolutely perfect. I don't know what to say. I just can't accept it as it is, however. Here, I have four dollars in my purse. Please take them so I'll know I've done my part to earn this ring."

It would ruin the moment, wouldn't it? The whole point of the gift is that it is received as a gift and not a purchase. Perhaps the simplest explanation of the gospel of Jesus Christ is found in John 3:16, "For God so loved the world that he gave his one and only Son, that whoever believes in him shall not perish but have eternal life."

Your Defining Moment

If the two of you have never made this decision to trust Christ alone for your salvation, do so today. It will prove to be the defining moment in your lives and marriage. Regardless of the hurt, pain, or sin that's part of your life's story, you will now be in God's eyes a brand new person, "Therefore, if anyone is in Christ, he is a new creation; the old has gone, the new has come! All this is from God, who reconciled us to himself through Christ" (2 Corinthians 5:17-18).

The two of you will have all the resources of heaven to confront the difficult spiritual, emotional, and relational issues in your lives. You will have an unending source of love, power, and strength you never possessed on your own.

There may still be work to be done in your hearts to deal with the emotional pain and scars you've experienced in life. There may still be effort needed to remove the resentments and bitterness you may have developed toward those who hurt you. But in your newfound relationship with Christ, you will discover the strength and grace to enable you to do what you once thought impossible—to forgive each other and soften your hearts toward each other.

The apostle Paul makes a wonderful confession in Philippians 4:13, "I can do everything through him who gives me strength." With Jesus Christ at the center of your lives, you likewise can discover that there are no problems, no heartaches, and no difficulties that ultimately the two of you cannot resolve. Jesus is the Friend of broken hearts...and

CHAPTER 4

A Hardened Heart:
The Master of Disguise

JIM AND SANDY SAT FACING AWAY from each other, arms crossed and faces grim. Though married for over twenty-five years, neither displayed even the slightest hint of affection for the other. She complained he was boring and took all the fun out of life. He shot back that she was a control freak and never listened to a word he said. Things were at a crisis for the two of them. He had just announced that as soon as he could get a new job, he was leaving her and moving out of state. When I (Bob) asked how long they had carried these hard feelings toward each other, they said for most of their married life.

It's amazing how long people will live in a cold, distant, and unful-filling marriage yet refuse to do anything about it. Well, that's not an entirely accurate statement. Usually they are willing to do something about it—the something is to blame the other person for the stale-mate (stale-mate: interesting term for marriage isn't it?). What Jim and Sandy had failed to consider in all their hurt and anger is the possibility that their own heart was the primary problem—and not the other person.

If Only My Spouse Would Change

The instinct to blame the other person for our pain goes as far back as the Garden of Eden. When God confronted Adam about his sin of eating the forbidden fruit, the very first husband replied, "The woman you put here with me—she gave me some fruit from the tree, and I ate it" (Genesis 3:12).

Notice Adam is even blaming God for part of the problem, "The woman you put here with me." It's part of our fallen human nature to point the finger at someone besides ourselves when things go wrong. That leads husbands and wives to conclude, "If only my spouse would just change, our marriage would work." Spouses are rarely being dishonest or deceptive when they accuse the other person of being the problem in their marriage. They believe with all their heart and soul that the only thing standing between them and a life of wedded bliss is their awful mate. "If only my loser spouse would change, then we could live happily ever after."

The problem with that thinking is that it leads to a dead end—and a hardened heart. We have never seen a marriage where only one partner needed to change. Or as the old adage says, "No matter how thin the pancake, it always has two sides."

You Take the Wall in Your Heart with You

Why isn't change in the other person enough to fix a marriage? The answer is simple: If I have a wall inside my heart built of pain and sin that blocks my ability to give and receive love, what difference will it make if my spouse changes? They could morph into a perfect human able to meet my every need, and I'd still have the same wall in my heart.

Even if you change spouses a dozen times, you will still have the same wall in your heart with Spouse #12 that you had with Spouse #1. That's why divorce, infidelity, swapping partners, and everything else people have tried never solves the problem. The wall in my heart won't go away just because I send my spouse away or because I find someone new. But try telling that to people who are convinced that their new lover or new marriage is the solution to all their pain.

Yet ask that person who has gotten a divorce if the exit of their first spouse took down the wall in their heart. There may be exceptions, but what we've heard time and again (and the statistics for the higher failure rate of second marriages bears this out) is that dissolving a marriage does little or nothing to resolve personal heart problems. In most cases, it only adds new problems to deal with.

Of all the words to use to describe divorce, infidelity, or an armed truce, the best one is this—*unnecessary.* It's unnecessary to end my marriage if my goal is to take down the wall in my heart. And only Jesus can take down that wall when I let Him heal the pain and forgive my sins.

Therefore, as difficult as my spouse might be, and as wrong as his or her behavior might be, positive change will never happen in our relationship until it happens first in my own heart.

Irrational Thinking

That I must change my own heart first if my spouse is to change her heart is a timeless and enduring principle of marriage. It is a fact of life that only an all-wise and all-loving God could weave into the divine fabric of relationships.

If you are unhappy in your marriage, that unhappiness has not been forced on you by your mate. It's something you have brought upon yourself by the view you have taken of your partner. Were you to adopt a different view of life and the world and change your attitude, you would no longer live each day in misery even if your spouse remains a difficult person.

It's reminiscent of the old adage, "Pain is inevitable but misery is optional." I can't stop pain from entering my life, but I can stop that pain from controlling my life. If I soften my heart toward my spouse, even if the pain in my marriage continues, it no longer has to control my life and attitude. If I can change how I respond to my partner, the misery I've lived with can come to an end.

The Power of a Changed Perspective

How we view our circumstances can have a tremendous sway over our emotional well-being. I (Bob) remember as a pastor calling on a woman dying of cancer. Her sister was taking care of her, and she was under hospice care. Her room was filled with the smell of various medications, and an oxygen machine was thumping away in the corner to help her breathe. The sense of impending death was in the room.

Yet, as I sat down to talk with her, I encountered someone with an incredibly upbeat attitude. "How are you today, Pastor? It's so good to see you. Tell me what's been going on at church. How is your family? Is there something I can pray about for you and your family?" Rather than focusing on her pain and grim prognosis, she focused with genuine interest on me. Strange as this may sound, every time I visited her I went away with a newfound joy in my heart. She inevitably lifted my spirits rather than the other way around.

Though she had real pain in her life, she chose not to exercise the misery option. As a result it changed the nature of her every conversation from gloom to joy.

Once You Change, Everything Changes

Here's a reality that may be difficult to swallow, but it could hold the key to the turnaround in your marriage: *If I soften my heart, then my marriage will start to change because I've changed.* We're not saying the problems in your marriage will instantly go away or that your spouse will experience a dramatic transformation. The truth is they could remain just as stubborn or even get worse. That's because we really have no control over what the other person does, just over how we will react to them.

What we can guarantee is that the chemistry of your relationship will change when you soften your heart. How? Even if your spouse steps on your pain, it will no longer control you—you are now free to choose your response. The misery and anger you felt for so long can be replaced by a new sense of peace and joy that comes from a softened heart.

That brings us back to a truth we started this chapter with. *If my marriage relationship is to change for the better, I have to choose to soften my heart first.*

The Cross Wasn't Fair

"Why should I have to take the first step if it's my spouse and not me with the major league problems? It's not fair."

We wish we had a good answer for that complaint. All we can say is that if you insist on fairness before you make any changes in your life, you will inevitably end up sad and disillusioned. Life is seldom fair. That's what heaven is for. Heaven is the place where all life's unfairness will be made fair. Until then, if you are going to make progress in your marriage, you will have to temporarily set aside your notion of fairness and do what will ultimately change hearts.

Before you are tempted to launch into a rant over how unfair life is, it would be good to remember this: Jesus—the only innocent and sinless person who ever lived—took on Himself the guilt, shame, and sin of the entire world. He was punished for all the things He didn't do in order that we could receive the forgiveness we didn't deserve. How unfair is that?

The apostle Paul writes, "God made him who had no sin to be sin for us, so that in him we might become the righteousness of God" (2 Corinthians 5:21). There simply never was nor ever will be anything as unfair as the cross, yet Jesus willingly embraced it in order to establish a relationship with us.

The prophet Isaiah saw the truth of this "unfair transaction" centuries earlier when he predicted the life of Christ,

> We all, like sheep, have gone astray,
>   each of us has turned to his own way;

> and the LORD has laid on him
> the iniquity of us all.
>
> (Isaiah 53:6)

God recognizes that only by extending His grace to us, rather than exacting His justice from us, can we be reconciled to Him.

The same is true in marriage. Only when we extend grace to our spouse, grace they may not deserve, can our hearts once again be connected in love. That's why I have to take the first step in softening my heart if the marriage is going to be healed. One partner can be faithful while the other is unfaithful, one sincere while the other is dishonest. One can be highly motivated to save the marriage while the other couldn't care less. Yet, rarely will assessing and assigning blame and demanding fairness solve problems in a marriage or change people's hearts. Looking for who is mainly at fault usually only hardens each person's heart.

The Speck in My Own Eye

What will work (though it may go against the grain of fairness) is for both spouses to look for ways they could soften their heart toward the other. Someone once said, "The biggest room in the world is the room for improvement in my own life."

Jesus teaches it's a better use of time to examine our own hearts rather than spend our time in finger-pointing: "Why do you look at the speck of sawdust in your brother's eye and pay no attention to the plank in your own eye? How can you say to your brother, 'Let me take the speck out of your eye,' when all the time there is a plank in your own eye?" (Matthew 7:3-4). Jesus also teaches that we all have enough areas of imperfection and needed growth in our lives that we should focus there first before we target the shortcomings of others. It's another way of stating this enduring truth: *If things are going to change in my marriage, the change needs to start with me.*

Why do we resist this truth at all costs—even to the point of losing our marriage? Why are we more eager to rush to judgment rather than take the first step to end the loneliness, anger, and detachment in our marriage?

The likely answer is pride. Pride creates spiritual blindness in our hearts. It gives us perfect 20/20 vision when it comes to seeing our spouse's faults, yet we have almost total nearsightedness when it comes to seeing our own heart problems. Jesus saw that problem at work among the people of His day:

> "'For this people's heart has become calloused;
>> they hardly hear with their ears,
>> and they have closed their eyes.
>
> Otherwise they might see with their eyes,
>> hear with their ears,
>> understand with their hearts
> and turn, and I would heal them.'"
>
> (Matthew 13:15)

THE MANY DISGUISES OF A HARDENED HEART

How do we close our eyes so that we cannot see the hardness of our own heart? Typically, we dress it up to look or sound like something other than what it is. We call it by a different name, use a euphemism, to mask its true identity.

Let's look at some of the most popular euphemisms to cover over the reality of a hardened heart.

Failed Communication

There are undoubtedly many others out there, but let's start with this one: *"We have a failure to communicate."*

Couples who can't quit bickering often use this as their excuse. Actually, couples who constantly pick at each other are often surprisingly clear and precise in their communication. Each understands exactly what the other person is saying. Consider this one barbed exchange we overheard in a public setting:

"Have you called our son yet?"

"Of course, don't you think I can remember his number?"

"I know you know his number. I was just asking if you had called him yet."

"You never believe me when I tell you I just did something. Do you think I'm lying to you?"

"No, you're just being difficult as usual."

Appearances to the contrary this is not a failure to communicate. It is an example of two people sending each other completely static-free messages, "I don't like you. In fact, I really don't like you. I wish you lived in Antarctica."

Apparently the love they felt for one another at some earlier time has morphed into utter contempt. It reminds me of the life cycle of married romance observed some two hundred years ago by British author (and cynic) Samuel Johnson (we've added our updated paraphrase in parentheses):

> Such is the common process of marriage (this is how life goes down, dude). A youth and maiden exchange meeting by chance, or are brought together by artifice (a blind date or an e-Harmony software glitch), exchange glances, reciprocate civilities (hit on each other), go home, and dream of each other (fall in love with love). Having little to divert attention (they each have no life), or diversify thought (brain freeze), they find themselves uneasy when they are apart, and therefore conclude that they shall be happy together (a state of temporary insanity called infatuation). They marry, and discover what nothing but voluntary blindness had before concealed (they get real); they wear out life in altercations (they fight like junkyard dogs), and charge

nature with cruelty. (Life is so unfair. Why me? Where's the number of the closest singles bar?)

Johnson's jaded description of love and marriage is unfortunately true for far too many couples. What was once white-hot infatuation is now stone-cold contempt.

How do we change from saying ugly things to each other to once again speaking words of love and tenderness? The first step is to soften our heart toward our spouse. For as Jesus made clear, it is in the heart that ugly and hurtful words find their genesis, "For from within, out of men's hearts, come evil thoughts, sexual immorality, theft, murder, adultery, greed, malice, deceit, lewdness, envy, slander, arrogance and folly. All these evils come from inside and make a man 'unclean'" (Mark 7:20-23).

It's not that most couples have a failure to communicate. They have a failure *to love each other from the heart.*

Different Values

This leads us to the second euphemism for a hardened heart: *"We don't share the same values."*

The reason many couples claim they cannot get along is that they just don't share the same core beliefs and convictions. Again, we beg to differ. The reality is not so much that a Grand Canyon-sized gulf exists in their values system, as much as they have hardened their hearts and chosen to disagree as a way of life.

The root cause is an inner decision to reject the other person from the heart. Once we decide we don't like the other person, or insist that we have to have our own way, even the smallest disagreements become impassable blockades.

If you don't believe conflicting values is often a disguise for a hardened heart, then consider how easy it becomes for two people to share the same values once they soften their hearts.

One of my (Bob's) favorite devotional writers from the early twentieth century tells the true story of a husband and wife who argued daily over what radio program to listen to. Finally they realized the problem was not their taste but the condition of their hearts. One afternoon when the wife's favorite program came on, she unexpectedly got up out of her chair and said, "Let's listen to your program instead." She turned to his station and sat down. The husband immediately jumped up from his chair and switched back to her program. Once their hearts had changed, so did their stations. Their clash of values was replaced by a desire to live in harmony and serve the other person.

The Bible describes this softening of our hearts this way,

> If you have any encouragement from being united with Christ, if any comfort from his love, if any fellowship with the Spirit, if any tenderness and compassion, then make my joy complete by being like-minded, having the same love, being one in spirit and purpose. Do nothing out of selfish ambition or vain conceit, but in humility consider others better than yourselves. Each of you should look not only to your own interests, but also to the interests of others (Philippians 2:1-4).

Couples who say they don't share the same values are often really saying, "We have closed our hearts toward each other. That's why we can't agree on anything." The answer is not to debate, argue, or coerce your spouse to accept your point of view. The answer is to let God soften both your hearts so that you become "like-minded, having the same love, being one in spirit and purpose."

Grown Apart

This brings us to our third disguise or euphemism for a hardened heart: *"We're no longer the same people. We've changed and grown apart."*

The story line to justify a divorce often goes like this, "We were too young when we got married—we really didn't know what we were doing. We're different people now than when we first met. It's just not fair to enforce a fifty-year marriage contract on kids in their early twenties. Our marriage is holding each of us back. It's time we admit the mistake and move on with our lives."

It sounds convincing at first, doesn't it? Not really. It's total and complete jive. A more honest statement would go like this: *"We have each hardened our hearts toward each other, we have no intention of changing, and we're looking for a good excuse to get out of this marriage."*

I (Bob) once spent time with a couple where the husband was seeking a divorce after nearly twenty-five years of marriage. He had found a new lover and was looking for cover to get out of the marriage. What was his alibi? He claimed their decision to get married in the first place was nothing more than "raging hormones."

Let's see, he was the victim of raging hormones? Is that anything like the raging bulls that stampede down the narrow streets of Pamplona, Spain, each year as young and foolish men attempt to outrun them? Is that what happened to this man? Apparently he wants me to believe that he was walking innocently across his college campus, when all of a sudden the cafeteria doors exploded and out rushed raging hormones. He tried to run for cover, but they caught up with him, gored his common sense, and trampled his character. They left him dazed and unable to exercise self-control. That's when he and his girlfriend decided to get married—they knew the raging hormones simply couldn't be outrun.

Now maybe you buy his story, but we don't. His marriage was not the result of irresistible circumstances or physiological drives beyond his control. If he became sexually involved with his girlfriend, it was his sinful human nature, not his testosterone, that got the better of him. The book of James tells us, "but each one is tempted when, by his own evil desire, he is dragged away and enticed. Then, after desire has conceived, it gives birth to sin; and sin, when it is full-grown, gives birth to death" (James 1:14-15).

He may have allowed his hormones to dictate his decision-making, but there was nothing inevitable about that. It was a choice he made in his heart, just as now it's a decision of his hardened heart to abandon the wife of his youth and engage in the ultimate selfish behavior—an extramarital affair.

Just Kidding

A fourth euphemism for a hardened heart is: *"Hey, I didn't mean anything by that. I was just teasing. You're way too sensitive."*

A hardened heart is often disguised as a sarcastic tongue. You hear them all the time—the jibes and put-downs people make about the person they are married to.

Yes, the one-liners can be funny. But when one or both spouses trade verbal barbs all day, it's a sure sign something deeper is wrong. Jesus said the most reliable way to determine the condition of someone's heart is to listen to what they say: "You brood of vipers, how can you who are evil say anything good? For out of the overflow of the heart the mouth speaks. The good man brings good things out of the good stored up in him, and the evil man brings evil things out of the evil stored up in him" (Matthew 12:34-35).

The words of a spouse with a hardened heart are a dead giveaway. They include unrelenting criticism, biting sarcasm, targeted put-downs, and words intended to wound. Late-night stand-up comedians owe much of their living to cynical marriage humor.

From our mouths we see what's really in our hearts. Despite what your spouse might say, teasing usually isn't all innocent fun. Sarcasm is anger with a smile. It's a passive-aggressive form of anger. It's one reason Paul warned the Ephesians (who were having their own relationship problems), "Do not let any unwholesome talk come from your mouths, but only what is helpful for building others up according to their needs, that it may benefit those who listen" (Ephesians 4:29).

The way we talk to our spouse can be a disguise for the fact our heart is hardening. The words we use reveal the condition of our heart. When our daily interchanges are filled with put-downs, criticisms, and sarcastic comebacks, it's fair to say something's wrong deep down inside.

Our mean-spirited words to each other hurt not only our marriage, but God Himself. That's why Paul cautions the Ephesians, "And do not grieve the Holy Spirit of God, with whom you were sealed for the day of redemption. Get rid of all bitterness, rage and anger, brawling and slander, along with every form of malice" (Ephesians 4:30-31).

Did you catch that? Whenever we, as believers, use our mouths to hurt, tear down, or attack our spouse, we grieve the Holy Spirit who lives in both of us.

Anger

This leads to another euphemism for a hardened heart: *"You make me so angry."*

The truth of the matter is no one can make us do something we don't want to do, including getting angry—not unless they have a gun pointed at our head. When we accuse someone else of making us angry, we are really saying that we've chosen in our hearts to get angry, and they are the excuse for doing so. Whatever the provocation, we ultimately make the call to respond with hostility and heated emotions. Our spouse doesn't get us mad; we decide to do that all on our own. This much is also certain—unhealthy and sinful anger is a sure-fire way to destroy intimacy and connectedness in a marriage.

The Bible warns about letting anger control our lives and relationships, "Everyone should be quick to listen, slow to speak and slow to become angry, for man's anger does not bring about the righteous life that God desires. Therefore, get rid of all moral filth and the evil that is so prevalent and humbly accept the word planted in you, which can save you" (James 1:19-21).

That's one reason we don't believe in anger management (at least for unhealthy anger). The Scriptures never tell us to manage our sinful anger. It instructs us to get rid of it, the way we should get rid of any other moral filth in our lives. Anger management doesn't make any more sense than hate management or lust management. You don't manage sin, you get rid of it.

Common Forms of Destructive Anger
· ·

When we allow sinful anger to make its home in our heart, it begins to harden it. Soon, our words are filled with sarcasm, put-downs, even abuse. But not all anger comes out as nasty words or mean-spirited jabs. Destructive anger toward our spouse can show itself in our attitudes or actions as well. Let's take a look at a few of the more common subterranean forms of simmering anger in a marriage.

Playing the Sculptor

When we play the sculptor, it means we're trying to change our spouse. Why are we trying to change them? We don't like them the way they are. We believe it's our calling (and right) to remake him or her. So we constantly chisel away trying to make our spouse more to our liking.

During our marriage conference, we usually ask the following questions, "Please don't raise your hands, but how many of you have been trying to change your spouse? How's that working for you? Almost finished? Or are you pretty much back where you started?" After the nervous laughter dies down, we then ask, "Please don't raise your hands, but how many of you enjoy being someone else's project?"

We often look at couples and say, "We have good news for you. If you think it's your job to change your spouse, you're fired. That's right. It's pink slip time. You've been laid off. What will you do with all that time you used to spend on changing your spouse? You can use it to change your own life. For most of us, at least, that's a full-time job."

There's a problem with playing the sculptor. Even if we are successful in changing our spouse (we've yet to meet someone who was), we face a bigger problem than the one we started with. Once we've changed our spouse, they now not only have their set of problems, but ours as well. We've remade them in our own image. And that's a tragic mistake.

Playing the sculptor is motivated by pride and a strong element of anger. We've yet to meet anyone working to remake their spouse who was not at least irritated, if not worse, with their spouse's personality traits. Try to hide it as they may, the anger in their relationship drips out like seeping water from limestone walls in a cave.

Playing the sculptor often comes out as reprimanding our mate for poor manners, showing disgust at their housecleaning skills, or comparing them unfavorably with members of our family. In worst case scenarios, it becomes intimidation or physical or emotional abuse.

We can't find anywhere in the Scriptures where we are commanded to change the person we're married to. There's a reason for that. The only person capable of changing a human heart is God Himself. So if either of you has labored all these years to change your spouse, here's your new job description. Accept your spouse just as they are, give thanks daily for the person God made them, and go to work full-time repairing your own shortcomings.

In other words, *soften your heart, let go of your anger, and start enjoying the person God gave you.* You will see immediate results as you begin to experience a new joy and contentment in your marriage.

Emotional Window-Shopping

Another form of simmering anger from a hardened heart is scanning the environment for a more appealing mate. We glance across the office and notice the well-dressed, smart, and confident woman, and we think, "She would make a terrific wife." Or we stare at the lead male singer with the vibrant smile and natural charisma and think, "I wish I had a husband like that." Emotional window-shopping rarely produces an affair at first. Rather, we use it to test the idea that someone other than our spouse would make us a happier person.

Inevitably, a comparison between someone we don't know that well and our all-too-familiar spouse leaves our partner weighed in the balance and found wanting. Given enough time, this dangerous daydreaming will move to the next stage. That's the day when temptation meets opportunity and the emotional window-shopping leads to an actual purchase. The devil will make sure the doors are wide open and the merchandise available at bargain prices.

One sure defense against falling into the infidelity trap is to shut down the window-shopping the moment it begins. The apostle Paul warns us, "Flee from sexual immorality. All other sins a man commits are outside his body, but he who sins sexually sins against his own body" (1 Corinthians 6:18). Perhaps the most effective strategy to avoid falling into adultery is to get rid of the anger in your heart toward your spouse. Emotional window-shopping loses all its appeal the moment we soften our heart toward our spouse and release the resentment and anger that led us to consider other people for a life partner.

Leveraging Our Love

Another form of a hardened heart is withholding our affection and love (including sex) from our mate until they meet our subjective and predetermined standards.

When we get angry with our spouse, we can decide to use whatever tools are available to us to make them change their ways. We call this leveraging our love because we are using our love (or sexual availability) to manipulate them to do what we want them to do. Statements such as, "When you get a better job, I'll start respecting you," "When you lose fifty pounds, I'll start showing interest in making love again," and "When you get your mother out of our marriage, I'll start speaking to you again," are all examples of leveraging our love.

Using our love as a bargaining chip is wrong. Love in marriage was never intended to be a tool for blackmail or manipulation. It goes against the very definition of love found in 1 Corinthians 13, "Love is patient, love is kind. It does not envy, it does not boast, it is not proud. It is not rude, it is not self-seeking, it is not easily angered, it keeps no record of wrongs" (vv. 4-5).

Did you catch that? Love is never self-seeking. Leveraging your love is the height of self-seeking behavior. Once we play that card, we engender resentment and bitterness in our spouse. Worse yet, our mate may decide that two can play this nasty game and start introducing their own form of emotional blackmail.

The biblical remedy to leveraging love is to soften our hearts and offer our spouse unconditional love. Unselfish love is described in Romans 15:7, "Accept one another, then, just as Christ accepted you, in order to bring praise to God." The apostle Paul specifically directs husbands to this lofty standard of sacrificial love in marriage: "Husbands, love your wives, just as Christ loved the church and gave himself up for her" (Ephesians 5:25).

What if Christ had leveraged His love for us? Where would we be today or for eternity? Imagine if He had said to us, "I won't accept you until you make certain changes in your life. If you can just get it together, if you get rid of the things I don't like, then I'll consider forgiving you and maybe offering you the gift of eternal life. But not until I see what I want to see."

Where would any of us be?

The Courtroom of Heaven

God's unconditional love is illustrated by a story evangelist Greg Laurie told at a men's conference.

Imagine it's the courtroom of heaven. God Almighty is the Judge, the devil is prosecutor, and you are the defendant. The devil, with great flourish and drama, begins his opening arguments against you by reminding the court that the very day you entered the world, you were stained by sin's ugly mark on your soul.

With a wicked smile, he starts to go one by one through all the awful and reprehensible things you thought, said, and did that are offensive in the eyes of a holy God.

He has so many examples to present that additional file cabinets must be brought into the courtroom. What began as a day of accusing testimony turns into weeks, then months of damning evidence that proves you have flouted the moral laws of God.

Months later the day finally arrives when the evil prosecutor sums up his case against you. "In conclusion, Your Honor, Your so-called Bible says quite plainly, 'The soul that sins shall die.'" He then whirls around and points his finger at you and shouts, "I have proven to this court beyond a reasonable doubt that this man has sinned countless times in his life. This court has no alternative but to declare that this miserable, pathetic human is guilty as charged. The holiness of heaven requires that you find him guilty and impose on him the ultimate punishment this court can impose—eternal death and separation! Your Honor, I rest my case."

The Judge looks over to your table. "Does the defense have any evidence to present?"

Your defense attorney, Jesus Christ, rises slowly from His chair and looks over the courtroom. After a moment He quietly says, "Your Honor, we have no evidence we can present to prove my client's innocence. My client is guilty as charged on all counts."

The devil jumps to his feet and shouts, "That's it! It's over! I've won!"

You slump in your chair, your attorney having just sealed your fate.

"Your Honor, may I approach the bench?" Jesus says.

The Almighty nods, and Jesus walks up to the bench. "Your Honor, may I remind this court of certain facts relevant to My client's defense?"

"Proceed."

Jesus turns and faces the courtroom. "You will remember, Your Honor, at a point in human history I got up from My throne in the glory of heaven. I willingly became a single cell placed in the womb of a young Jewish virgin who lived in Nazareth. Nine months later I was born in a humble stable in Bethlehem and then raised in the home of Joseph the carpenter.

"At age thirty I sensed Your call to public ministry and began by being baptized in the Jordan River by My cousin, John the Baptist. The moment I came up from the water, the Holy Spirit descended on

Me like a dove. That's when I heard Your voice, Your Honor, 'This is My Son, whom I love. With Him I am well-pleased.'

"For the next three years I went about doing good, healing the sick, feeding the hungry, and raising the dead to life. At the end of that time I was arrested on false charges, faced a mockery of a trial, and was sentenced to death for crimes I never committed.

"I hung upon a Roman cross for almost six hours, Your Honor. It was then You poured out on Me all Your holy wrath and hatred for sin. Hour after hour You rained down judgment for sin upon Me until My heart could take no more. At last I cried out, 'My God, My God, why have You forsaken Me?' At that moment You turned Your face away from Me, something I had never experienced in all of eternity.

"The pain of separation from Your Honor was more than I could bear. About the ninth hour of the day I opened My parched lips and cried out, 'It is finished.'"

"Objection, Your Honor!" the devil shouts. "This has absolutely no relevance to the matter at hand. The defense has already conceded guilt on the part of the defendant. Let's disperse with this irrelevant reminiscing and move immediately to the sentencing."

"If the Court will indulge Me," Jesus says, "I will prove that My story has true relevance to this case."

"Objection overruled," the Judge announces. "You may proceed with Your statement, Counselor."

"Thank You, Your Honor. With the weight of the entire world's sins upon My shoulders, My heart could take it no longer. I died, as You well know, of a broken heart. That's why blood and water flowed from My side when I was pierced by the soldier's spear."

At the mention of Jesus' blood, the devil winces and looks away.

"I was then laid in the borrowed tomb of a rich man. Soldiers were posted to make certain no one could steal My body. For two days I laid in the grave while My friends wept. But then"—a joyous smile spreads across Jesus' face—"but then, Your Honor, You raised Me from the dead!"

Immediately the angels sitting in the gallery cry out, "Hallelujah! He is risen! He is risen indeed!" The Judge nods in agreement, but motions for them to be seated. They obediently bow and sit down quietly in their seats.

The devil stands up once again. "This all may be well and good, Your Honor, but it has no relevance to the defendant. He has sinned, and the soul who sins shall die. I call for the verdict from this court to be rendered at once!"

"Your Honor," Jesus says, "this has everything to do with the case at hand. My resurrection was the seal of Your final approval on My life. It signaled You had accepted My suffering and death as the perfect sacrifice for My client's sins.

"The Court will recall that when my client was twelve years old, he heard and understood the gospel for the first time. One evening, following a message by an evangelist, he publicly acknowledged his need for the forgiveness of his sins. Overcoming his fears and doubts, he knelt at an altar and put his faith in what I had accomplished for him on the cross. That night My client received My unconditional gift of eternal life."

The devil turns away and chews on his fingernail.

"Therefore, Your Honor," Jesus says, "let the record show My client's sins have already been paid for—all of them. The sentence of death he justly deserves has already been carried out by this court. It was carried out on Me, on his behalf. The prosecutor himself knows the laws of heaven will not allow a man to be tried twice for the same crime. This court can only do what love and justice demand—declare My client 'Not Guilty' of any and all charges against him!"

The Judge slams down His gavel and thunders to the farthest reaches of the universe, "Case dismissed!"

That's what we mean when we say God's love is unconditional. The Bible says, "But God demonstrates his own love for us in this: While we were still sinners, Christ died for us" (Romans 5:8). If God is willing to go so far as to offer His Son as a sacrifice for us, how can we hold small grudges and grievances against our spouse? Leveraging our love is not something God does, nor should we.

Subtle Shunning

This final form of punishing anger against our mate is invisible for a few hours (or days). It's sometimes called "the silent treatment." It may involve refusing to talk to your spouse or failing to give eye contact at the table or even conveniently logging on to the Internet right after supper. It can take the form of refusing to hold your spouse's hand in public or just happening to forget their birthday or your anniversary.

The message of our subtle shunning is clear: "I'm so angry at you, I'm going to treat you as if you don't exist. Maybe then you'll wake up and admit you are wrong."

This, of course, directly contradicts the direction Scripture gives wives and husbands on how to treat each other. The apostle Peter advises, "Wives, in the same way be submissive to your husband so that, if any of them do not believe the word, they may be won over without words by the behavior of their wives, when they see the purity and reverence of your lives" (1 Peter 3:1-2). It's hard for wives to impress husbands with the purity and reverence of their lives when they are glaring at them across the dinner table.

Likewise, Peter tells husbands how they ought to treat their wives: "Husbands, in the same way be considerate as you live with your wives, and treat them with respect as the weaker partner and as heirs with you of the gracious gift of life, so that nothing will hinder your prayers" (1 Peter 3:7). It's hard to see how a husband can show consideration and respect for his wife when he refuses to answer her simplest questions or treats her as invisible.

When we demonstrate any of these hidden forms of anger, it's more evidence that we've hardened our heart toward our spouse. We need to remember our angry behavior doesn't go unnoticed by our heavenly Father. Out of love for us He will bring the conviction of the Holy Spirit into our lives, warning us of the damage we are doing to each other. If we are wise, we'll heed the warning and soften our heart toward our spouse.

Yet, if we resist over and over again, we can enter into a state of heart the Bible calls rebellion. It's rebellion not just against our mate but against God Himself. The writer of Hebrews warns,

> So, as the Holy Spirit says:
> "Today if you hear his voice,
>   do not harden your hearts
> as you did in the rebellion
>   during the time of testing in the desert…"
>
> (Hebrews 3:7-8)

Conclusion

The hardened heart is a master of disguise. It hides behind a number of euphemisms, all meant to conceal our basic problem—a hardened heart. While there may be a grain of truth in all these excuses for why we can't get along, the basis problem is a hardened heart caused by pride and rebellion.

Yet things can change. We can give up the excuses and truly humble ourselves before God and each other. There is a way back home to a loving and connected marriage, if we're willing to travel that road.

The yellow ribbon is a popular symbol for remembering various causes. It serves as a symbol of support for soldiers serving overseas, for missing children, and for fighting against serious illnesses. Yet the origin of the familiar symbol is quite different. It goes back to a popular song in the 1970s titled "Tie a Yellow Ribbon." The inspiration for the song came from the true story of a young man who fell in with the wrong crowd and ended up in prison. There, behind bars, the boy's heart was filled with remorse for the pain he had caused his family.

Shortly before he was to be paroled, he wrote to his parents apologizing for his behavior. He asked for their forgiveness. He said he would understand if they never wanted to see him again. He explained he would soon be released and take the bus home from prison. If his parents wanted him to get off, they should signal their intentions by tying a single yellow ribbon around the old oak tree in the front yard. However, if they could not forgive him, they should simply leave the tree unadorned.

On the day of his release he quietly climbed on the bus that would take him home. As he traveled ever closer toward his boyhood farm home, he could hardly stand the tension. He leaned over to the stranger seated next to him and asked, "Would you mind telling me if you see a single yellow ribbon tied to the next big oak tree?"

At first taken aback by the odd request, the stranger eventually consented. The young man then put his head down and waited—his stomach tied in knots.

When the moment of truth arrived, he couldn't take it any longer. "What do you see? Is there a yellow ribbon tied to the tree?"

"I'm afraid not," the stranger said. The boy's heart sank like a stone. The stranger continued, "What I see is about a hundred yellow ribbons tied around that tree."

The young man jerked his head up and looked out the bus window. The family tree was ablaze with yellow ribbons. There stood his parents in the driveway, with the family dog wagging his tail in anticipation. As the bus screeched to a halt and the door opened, the boy fell into his parents' arms.

The journey back to a loving and connected marriage begins when we undergo a genuine change of heart. Until then, all the euphemisms and attempts to disguise our hard hearts will keep us from experiencing true intimacy. As we'll see in the next chapter, the journey to a softened heart begins with a return to the way it was "in the beginning."

> *Lord Jesus, I've been tempted to believe that the problems in my marriage were primarily my spouse's fault. I've wanted them to change more than I've wanted to change. I realize that the*

real change needs to take place in my own heart. I ask Your forgiveness for being so quick to point out the sins and short-comings of others and so slow to recognize my own. Please show me all the ways that I may have disguised the hardness of my own heart. Give me a new desire and willingness to love my spouse as they deserve to be loved. Do whatever You have to do to change my heart so that it is like Your heart. Amen.

Questions for You and Your Spouse to Discuss

1. Why doesn't it work to wait for the other person to soften their heart first? Why do you have to give up on the idea of fairness if you are to connect your hearts?

2. Why is it an irrational idea for you to assume your happiness depends on some other person? How can you both be joyful living in a less than perfect world or marriage?

3. What's the danger in withholding love until you get what you want? Why is loving each other in an unconditional way so important in connecting your hearts?

CHAPTER 5

When God Does Open Heart Surgery

I (BOB) SAT IN THE UPPER DECK of one of America's truly great sports stadiums—the Georgia Dome—and marveled at the nearly fifty thousand men who surrounded me. It was an impressive sight. Men from all over America gathered over a Valentine's Day to learn, among other things, how to be better husbands (only men could have planned a conference on that date).

To make up for our absence from our wives, the male organizers did the next best thing—they handed out Valentine's Day cards for us to fill out. As I sat musing about what I should say to my dear wife back in Chicago (to justify why I wasn't there on Valentine's Day), something unexpected happened. The Holy Spirit made a visit to my row.

While I had intended to write something sentimental and safe, an Influence much stronger than my own began to redirect my thoughts. *You need to apologize to Cheryl for how hard you've been on her,* was the first impression my heart received. The impression continued, *You need to be specific in the areas you need to ask her forgiveness.*

I sat up and was now taking this whole card writing exercise much more seriously. The tenor of the note changed from "Okay, here's to prove I haven't forgotten you," to "I need to confess some things that I have done to hurt you."

A Simple Prayer That Changed My Life

By the time I was done with the card, it was filled with sincere, heartfelt words of apology on the bottom, top, and back sides. I remember looking up at the ceiling of the Georgia Dome as I licked the envelope and prayed, *Lord, please help me to love Cheryl even more than I do now. Please help me to be the husband I should be.*

I had no idea what that simple prayer would lead to.

Approximately two weeks after returning home from the big stadium event, Cheryl approached me with what I call her serious smile.

"Okay, what is it?" I assumed it was either the car not running right or the electric bill overdue.

"We're going to have a baby," she said calmly.

"Whose baby?" I asked. "And are we keeping it for the weekend?"

"I'm talking about our baby…you and I. We are going to have a baby."

"But…but we had our last baby nine years ago," I said. "Cheryl, we don't even own a stroller or crib any longer. We gave all those things away years ago."

"Then we'll have to get all new ones," Cheryl said.

That's when another thought hit me, one that sent chills down my spine. "Sweetheart…who is going to tell our parents?"

"I'm certainly not going to," Cheryl said. "You can."

"Oh, no, you can do that."

Several of our earlier pregnancies had been so physically difficult that both sets of grandparents were still overcome with exhaustion every time they even thought about those days. Here we were about to start all over again.

Admitted in Serious Condition

A few weeks later, after the initial shock subsided, a new obstacle presented itself—morning sickness. It wasn't long until Cheryl was throwing up eight, ten, twelve times a day. Meanwhile, I continued to work full-time at our church plus trying to be Dad to our four children. Running back and forth to fix dinner, wash clothes, and care for a bedridden Cheryl was, shall we say, a little taxing.

The menu possibilities that Cheryl could keep down continued to dwindle by the week. Eventually it was reduced to one item: a grape Mister Misty from Dairy Queen.

Finally, the day came when no longer even a grape Mister Misty worked. Home health nurses were called in to insert IV drips into her arm to keep her hydrated. Our neighbor Cecelia, a good friend and a nurse, kindly administered injections of anti-nausea medication twice a day. Still, these combined efforts ultimately proved to be of no avail. Cheryl was now throwing up twenty to thirty times a day.

One morning I came into our room to check on her when she weakly said, "Bob, I don't mean to alarm you...but this morning I saw a tunnel...a tunnel with a white light at the end."

That was it. I immediately loaded Cheryl into our van and raced off for our community hospital. After a brief stop in the emergency room, Cheryl was admitted to the hospital in serious condition.

Her diagnosis was serious dehydration and malnourishment, and the doctors initiated an intensive regimen of intravenous fluids. For the next several days we waited and prayed as these treatments slowly began to take effect. Finally, later in the week, the vomiting started to calm down. Cheryl started to show signs of recovery—even a slight appetite returned.

An Agonizing Dilemma

Believing the worst was behind us, I turned my full-time attention to keeping our home in order and taking care of the children. I was helping get the kids ready for school one morning when the phone rang.

"Hi, it's me," Cheryl said quietly.

"Hey, honey. How are you feeling today?"

"Well, not so good. I think I have a problem."

"What kind of problem?"

"Overnight my shoulder began to turn red and swell. So did my neck. It really hurts. The nurses won't say for sure, but they think I may have a blood clot."

"A blood clot. You're kidding. What do the doctors say?"

"They are concerned and have ordered tests. They say blood clots sometimes form where the feeding tube is inserted."

I wanted to remain calm for Cheryl's sake, but my heart was racing. "So if...if it is a blood clot, what will they do?"

"They said they'll start me on a blood thinner right away. But there's a problem with that too. The nurses say too much blood thinner and we could lose the baby—a spontaneous miscarriage. On the other hand, if the clot breaks loose..."

I knew just enough to understand that if a blood clot goes to her heart or lung...it's game over.

I hung up the phone a shaken man. I immediately called a nurse from our congregation and described the crisis. She was an emergency room nurse in a large hospital. She listened politely, then said in a firm voice, "If I were you, Bob, I would move Cheryl to a high-risk pregnancy unit at once. Small hospitals like yours aren't equipped to deal with situations like this one. I'd move her today."

A Desperate Call to Prayer

I thanked her for her advice and hung up the phone. I sank to my knees next to our bed and prayed, "O Lord, You have seen how hard I've tried to help Cheryl. You've seen how I've tried to keep our family together...and now this. O God, please help us."

At that moment I experienced the Influence I had felt at the Georgia Dome months earlier: "Call your friends who pray" was the simple message impressed on my heart. My mind went to different people from several churches we had served who had special ministries of prayer and intercession. These choice servants of God would often spend three, four, even five hours a day on their knees for others.

I picked up the phone and made one call after another to our praying friends—some who lived in a different state. As I explained the gravity of the situation, each one assured me they would take the matter to God right away. As I hung up after the last call, my spirit began to relax, and a strange sense of peace started to settle over my heart. While I had no idea how this was all going to end, I knew it was now in God's hands.

The Bright Spot on the Screen

That evening I visited Cheryl in the hospital for the second time that day, and she informed me she was being taken downstairs to undergo further testing. They wanted to continue watching the blood clot and determine if new clots had developed.

Cheryl was wheeled into a small room complete with sophisticated computerized instruments and screens. The ultrasound technicians first scanned the portion of Cheryl's neck, where they found the clot earlier in the day. A color image of her blood flow appeared on the screen including a tiny bright spot.

"That's the clot," one of the technicians informed me. "We'll look for others now."

I stood back as they methodically worked over the main arteries of Cheryl's neck. I must have been lost in thought because the next thing I realized was that a new tension had entered the room. The two technicians seemed to be arguing with each other as they adjusted dials on the computer console. Finally they made a joint decision to reboot the computer.

"Excuse me, but is there something wrong?" I asked.

"Please just stand back and let us do our job," one of the technicians said.

Yes, something was wrong.

That's Not the Way Things Work

The technicians were clearly upset. After several minutes of debating the meaning of the data they were seeing, they elected to shut off the machine again.

"Excuse me, but I would like to know what's going on," I said.

One of the technicians looked at me and said, "Okay, we'll tell you what's wrong. We can't find the blood clot."

"But…we just saw it on the screen a few moments ago."

"I know we did. That's why we're checking other areas to see what's happened to it."

Cheryl looked up from the table where she was lying and said quietly, "Maybe I've been healed."

"Oh, sure," one of the technicians scoffed. "I'll just wave a magic wand over you and make it go away. I'm sorry—but that's not the way things work."

Looking at Cheryl's peaceful face, I suddenly lost all my anxiety as well. We smiled at each other knowing something important had just happened. I leaned over and whispered, "I'm going home to put the children to bed. Call me when they know something definite."

"Give the children a kiss good-night for me," she said.

"I will. I love you."

"I love you too."

I exited the lab area and headed out to my car. We lived less than a mile from the hospital, so I was back in a matter of minutes to let the babysitter go home.

The four children greeted me at the door. "How's Mom?"

"She'll call in a little while and let us know," I said. "Come on, it's time for bed."

Introducing a Brand New Bride

Just as I was tucking the last of the children into bed, the phone rang.

"Hi, Bob, it's me," said the sweet voice on the other end.

"Well, what have they decided?"

"You can come get me."

"What—are you going over the wall?" My first thought was that she had decided to make a break for it under the cover of darkness.

"No, they're releasing me tonight. The radiologist was just here and read the results. He says there is no blood clot. As soon as the doctor on call signs off, I can go home. You can come get me."

Tears filled my eyes. I could hardly speak. "I'll be there in just a few minutes."

The day had started with urgent advice to move Cheryl to a high-risk pregnancy unit. Now it was ending with a doctor saying there was no reason for her to stay in the hospital. My mind went to all those people who had spent the day on their knees praying for our family. How could I ever thank them?

I no sooner put the phone down than I found our children standing in the hallway behind me.

"What's happening?" they asked, worried expressions on their faces.

"Get your coats on. We're going to get Mom and bring her home!"

"We are? Yeah! Yeah!" they squealed in unison.

In a matter of minutes we pulled our van in front of the hospital entrance. Cheryl was sitting inside the doorway in a wheelchair with a nurse standing beside her. As soon as she recognized our car, she broke out in a big smile. She even stood up under her own strength. We were soon on our way home with everyone safe and sound.

That night as Cheryl slept quietly beside me, I looked over and could not believe my eyes. The morning had begun with concern for her life and that of the baby. Now she was home and she was going to be all right.

The next Sunday Cheryl felt well enough to attend church with me. For months she had not felt well enough to go. It's a Sunday I will never forget. As we stood together after the service and shook hands with our parishioners, I had this strange feeling I was introducing everyone to my new bride.

A Final Question for My Heart

My heart was filled with wonder, gratitude, and a new sense of love for her. She was alive and so was our unborn child. That afternoon the same Influence that had spoken to my heart at the Georgia Dome returned with one more question for me.

Well, Bob, how do you feel about your wife now? Do you love her more than you did when you asked Me to change your heart?

My inner response was immediate, *Are You kidding? Of course I do. I've never been more grateful for her in my entire life.*

It then dawned on me what had happened—*God had softened my heart toward my wife.* He answered my prayer from the second deck of the Georgia Dome, yet He did so in a way I never could have foreseen.

Six months later a beautiful baby girl was born to our family. Two years later God graciously gave us our third daughter, MacKenzie. The four teenagers quickly fell in love with both little girls.

What It Takes

We share our story because we believe it illustrates an important principle. *God will do whatever He has to do to soften our hearts, if we allow Him to do so.*

Some of you reading this might be frightened off by that statement. Who in their right mind would ask God to put them through such a difficult and trying experience as ours? Just so I can get closer to my spouse? Would it really be worth it?

Those are good questions and deserve good answers.

To begin with, I didn't ask God to put me through a difficult experience. I only gave God permission to do whatever He needed to do to soften my heart. That same something He wants to do in your life could perhaps be accomplished through great blessing instead of a great trial. Only God knows what it will take to soften your heart.

God Disciplines Us for Our Good

Letting God soften our hearts is part of the discipline process the writer of Hebrews talks about,

> Endure hardship as discipline; God is treating you as sons. For what son is not disciplined by his father? If you are not disciplined (and everyone undergoes discipline), then you are illegitimate children and not true sons. Moreover, we have all had human fathers who disciplined us and we respected them for it. How much more should we submit to the Father of our spirits and live! (Hebrews 12:7-9).

The writer then explains the magnificent payoff for experiencing God's heart-changing work in our lives:

> Our fathers disciplined us for a little while as they thought best; but God disciplines us for our good, that we may share in his holiness. No discipline seems pleasant at the time, but painful. Later on, however, it produces a harvest of righteousness and peace for those who have been trained by it (12:10-11).

"No discipline seems pleasant at the time…" We found out that's sure true. Yet we also found this to be true: "Later on, however, [discipline] produces a harvest of righteousness and peace for those who have been trained by it."

God will not put us through difficulty or testing a single minute longer than we need in order for Him to soften our heart.

Your Grief Will Turn to Joy—It's a Promise

When God is through with the process of softening our hearts, the rewards to our marriage will far outweigh the costs. The "harvest of righteousness and peace" that Scripture promises is just one way of describing the new sense of love and intimacy you will share with your spouse. For me, it was the sense that our marriage had started all over again. I was now supremely thankful that my wife was still alive and that we had a future together.

Jesus teaches that enduring hardship brings lasting rewards of joy. On the very last evening of His life, He told His disciples,

> "I tell you the truth, you will weep and mourn while the world rejoices. You will grieve, but your grief will turn to joy. A woman giving birth to a child has pain because her time has come; but when her baby is born she forgets the anguish because of her joy that a child is born into the world. So with you: Now is your time of grief, but I will see you again and you will rejoice, and no one will take away your joy" (John 16:20-22).

If we give God permission to soften our hearts, we will also have to choose to trust Him come what may. This is not a reckless gamble or blind leap of faith. How can we know that? Because God's Word clearly tells us the Lord has only our good in mind: "Don't be deceived, my dear brothers. Every good and perfect gift is from above, coming down from the Father of the heavenly lights, who does not change like shifting shadows. He chose to give us birth through the word of truth, that we might be a kind of firstfruits of all he created" (James 1:16-18).

THE NEXT STEPS IN SOFTENING OUR HEARTS

In earlier chapters we learned how to discover what has hardened our hearts. Once we are aware of the issues, we are ready to take these next steps in softening our hearts toward our spouse.

Confession

The first step in softening our hearts: *We must confess each area of our hardness of heart to God and to our spouse.*

This crucial principle is explained in James 5:16: "Therefore confess your sins to each other and pray for each other so that you may be healed. The prayer of a righteous man is powerful and effective."

What Are True Confessions?

Let's begin to examine this step by talking about what confession is not. It is not a coerced admission of guilt extracted under unbearable pressure. Enemy captors often torture their prisoners to elicit "confessions" for propaganda purposes. Such coerced admissions of guilt in no way qualify as true biblical confessions. Nor is it a religious ritual where you rehearse your list of sins and wait for someone in spiritual authority to absolve you.

Biblical confession means to wholeheartedly agree with God and others that we have done something wrong. To soften our hearts toward our spouse will require us to agree with God and our husband or wife where we have acted wrongly.

Early in our marriage, I (Bob) took Cheryl to a class reunion at my college. She was eager to meet my friends and be introduced as my wife. Instead, when it came time to introduce us, I did my class clown routine and joked that I had come alone. It drew laughs, but all at Cheryl's expense. On the way home, she told me how deeply hurt she was by my "humor." I suddenly understood how foolishly I had behaved at her expense. I agreed with her that I had shown a lack of love and respect in front of my old classmates. I agreed with her it was wrong and should never happen again.

When Others Suffer Because of Our Hard Hearts

Confession involves a deep realization of the painful impact my sin has had on others (and myself). In a rather unusual story in the Old Testament (see 2 Samuel 24; 1 Chronicles 21), King David decides to count the number of fighting men available to him. But taking the census of his military might displeases God. As a result over seventy thousand innocent people are struck down in a three-day plague that decimates Israel.

Why such stern punishment? What's wrong with knowing how many soldiers are on active duty at the moment? The story does raise all sorts of theological questions, some of which are difficult to explain. Yet the central truth of the story is clear: David had developed a dangerous arrogance in his heart toward God—he was hardening his heart. By taking the census he revealed he was trusting in military might rather than in God's faithfulness and character.

David, the same man who once faced a nine-foot giant with only five stones and a slingshot, was now uneasy unless he knew how many soldiers he had under arms. Because of his unique position as king and spiritual leader of Israel, if David's heart went bad, the entire nation would likely go bad and perish. Thus the spiritual stakes were so enormously high that drastic intervention on God's part was required.

As the enormity of his sin and its devastating consequences on innocent people dawned on him, David's heart changed. "When David saw the angel who was striking down the people, he said to the LORD, 'I am the one who has sinned and done wrong. These are but sheep. What have they done? Let your hand fall upon me and my family'" (2 Samuel 24:17).

David's words, "I am the one who has sinned and done wrong," is the essence of confession. When we agree with God (and others) that we have done something sinful, we can experience not only forgiveness but healing (James 5:16). In marriage, confession opens the floodgates of heaven and allows God's mercy, grace, and healing power to come flowing down. Where there was once only indifference, anger, and distance in our hearts, confession irresistibly draws us back toward each other.

A Painful Secret Revealed

Jose and Juanita met and married in their late thirties. They both were committed Christians with high hopes for a Christ-centered marriage. They eventually decided to serve full-time in a Christian ministry in South America. Not wanting to jeopardize his fresh start in life, Jose chose to keep the unfortunate details of his life as a single man from his new wife. Both of them had come from troubled homes marked by over-control, abandonment, and a lack of love. The result was Juanita became an angry and dominating person. Jose, on the other hand, became a withdrawn and insecure person who could not express himself but was intensely angry on the inside.

It didn't take long for the trouble to start in their marriage. Every time Jose tried to express himself, Juanita would squelch his ideas or put him down. Feeling controlled by his wife but unable to assert himself, Jose alternated between angry outbursts and sullen retreats— even occasional threats of suicide. Meanwhile, Juanita increasingly felt unloved, isolated, and empty in their marriage.

During times when Jose felt crushing pressure from his domineering wife, he would sometimes shout, "If I'm such a bad person then maybe I should just end it all. That would make you happy." Juanita would collapse in tears and frustration as she simply could not understand why Jose (and her children) reacted to her in such a negative way. After all, she meant so well.

Finally the two sought out counseling to see if they could save their twenty-year marriage. During the week of counseling, a number of sin and emotional pain issues surfaced in their hearts. They realized how often they were stepping on each other's pain and further damaging each other's hearts. Once they saw the unloving and destructive pattern they were in, they began to engage in mutual confession and forgiveness.

Both made progress until the fourth day when the counselor asked them to confess their moral failures to God and each other. Jose agreed to go first. He had made a list of the serious moral transgressions that had occurred in his life before he met Juanita. She sat and listened in stunned disbelief as Jose revealed that he had lived with numerous women. He had never told her about this dark side of his past.

"You told me you had done some bad things before we met," she sobbed, "but never in a million years did I suspect this."

Jose looked down; it had taken a great deal of courage to reveal his dark secrets.

The couple left the office that morning with Juanita deeply upset and Jose uncertain if their marriage would survive. They sat in the front seat of their SUV for several more hours outside the counseling office engaged in intense discussion. Had Jose made a huge mistake by openly confessing his previous wrongdoing to his wife? Would it have been better just to continue hiding the truth?

Confession and Renunciation Bring Mercy

The next morning Jose and Juanita appeared at the counselor's office as scheduled. This time things were different—very different. They were smiling, holding hands, and looking relaxed. They moved their chairs as close as they could to each other. Jose was animated and talked more in the first hour than he had all week. Meanwhile, Juanita sat staring adoringly as her husband shared what God had taught him that morning in his personal devotions.

What in the world happened? How did a couple go from constant bickering and threats of suicide to acting like newlyweds? The answer is confession. Confession had broken down the barriers that had blocked their hearts and relationship for decades. For the first time in their marriage, they were experiencing a true heart connection. That's really no surprise. The Bible promises,

> He who conceals his sins does not prosper,
>   but whoever confesses and renounces them finds mercy.
>
> (Proverbs 28:13)

When Jose showed the courage to openly confess his sins to God and his wife, the invisible wall in his heart blocking intimacy suffered a total collapse. His willingness to be honest and open with her ultimately allowed God to soften his heart and the heart of his wife.

Our past sexual behavior may not be the only area where we need to engage in confession and renunciation. What about the cruel and heartless things we've said to our spouse? What about the deep and bitter feelings we've harbored toward their family? What about our years of prideful self-focus where we made our own needs and goals the center of the marriage?

Forgiveness

Not only is honest confession needed to soften our hearts, but so is forgiveness. In many respects it may involve the most difficult choices we'll ever make: *To soften our heart we must choose to forgive everyone who has hurt us.*

Forgiveness is the other side of confession. While in confession we agree we owe others a moral debt and ask to be released from it, in forgiveness we agree others owe us a moral debt and agree to free them from their obligation.

Jesus teaches this concept of indebtedness to others and the necessity of cancelling those debts in the parable of the unmerciful servant (Matthew 18:23-35). In that story a king is ready to settle accounts with all his servants. A man who owes ten thousand talents (equivalent to several billion dollars in today's economy) is brought before him and begs for more time. The king takes pity on him and cancels the entire amount and lets him go free.

But the story doesn't end there. The newly freed servant finds someone on the street who owes him less than a few months' wages. When that man can't pay up, the unmerciful servant grabs him and starts to choke him, demanding his money now. The poor man begs for patience, but the hard-hearted servant throws him into debtor's prison and leaves him there to rot until he can repay.

The king learns of this distressing turn of events. He calls the man in and asks, "Shouldn't you have had mercy on your fellow servant just as I had on you?" (v. 33). This time the king is not so lenient. He orders his jailers to imprison and torture the man until he pays back the several billion he owes.

Jesus concludes by saying the story has little to do with money but everything to do with our heart attitude: "This is how my heavenly Father will treat each of you unless you forgive your brother from your heart" (v. 35).

When our spouse says something sarcastic, they are in our moral debt. When we glare with hateful thoughts at our mate, we are in their moral debt. Whenever we sin against each other in marriage, we now owe the other person something. We have taken from them trust, self-respect, dignity, peace of mind, and integrity, among other things.

Now the relationship can be restored only if the debt is repaid or if it is cancelled altogether. Justice demands debt repayment. Mercy allows debt cancellation. Jesus tells us when we forgive another person "from our heart," we have released them from all their obligations to repay us. It's as if the bank holding our seriously overdue Visa card account were to suddenly wipe out all our consumer debt. It would be a display of mercy, not justice.

All of us owe God billions and billions in moral debts we cannot repay. However, through the cross of Jesus Christ that debt has been completely cancelled. Now our obligation is to release our spouse from whatever moral debts they might owe us. In comparison to what we once owed God, what our mate still owes us is only a pittance.

The Basics of True Forgiveness

John Regier has practical insights into why forgiveness is so necessary if we are to soften our hearts toward our spouse:

> Circumstances and relationships have hurt each of us; bitterness is a tool of Satan to defeat believers; Scripture warns against bitterness; the cure for bitterness is forgiveness; and forgiveness demands a payment. True forgiveness involves (1) a choice—the person who has been wronged can choose to forgive or not to forgive; (2) releasing—it is the voluntary

act of releasing someone from the emotional damage caused by his sin and no longer holding him responsible for the consequences of that failure; (3) substitution—one person pays for the emotional pain that another caused. In doing so, the debt of emotional damage is paid (assumed).[2]

Can forgiveness actually prove to be the breakthrough a badly wounded marriage needs?

One day an angry couple sat in my (Bob's) office several feet away from each other. I learned in talking with them that Antwon was emotionally distant and detached from Felicia. He would often walk away from an argument and pretend she didn't exist. Felicia would follow him out of the room, bombarding him with verbal assaults in a desperate attempt to get his attention. As a result she struggled with a sense of rejection and fear of opening her heart to him lest she be hurt again. As far as they saw things, the only question on the table was how to expedite their inevitable divorce.

Yet as they begin to pray through the sheets I gave them, on which I had listed the way other people, their family, and their spouse had hurt them, things began to change.

"Lord, I choose to forgive Felicia for judging me," Antwon read from his paper, "and for verbally attacking me, leaving me feeling disrespected and not valued." He then read the prayer at the bottom of the page, "I choose to release Felicia from the moral debt she owes me. I agree to pay the price for the emotional consequences this caused. I take back the ground I gave to the enemy through my bitterness, and I yield it to the Lord Jesus Christ."

One by one, Antwon read through the list of the ways Felicia had hurt him and the negative emotions it had caused. He followed that with a prayer of release, and as he did so, the tension and worried lines on his face began to ease.

Next it was Felicia's turn to forgive. "Lord, I choose to forgive Antwon for refusing to talk to me when I'm hurting and simply walking away, leaving me to feel abandoned and uncared for. I choose to release Antwon from the moral debt he owes me, and I agree to pay the price for the emotional consequences his sin caused."

Forgiveness Works Regardless of the Temperature

As she prayed through her list of items, tears began to roll down her cheeks. When she was done, the two looked at each other—and smiled. Forgiveness had removed huge barriers in their hearts, and the new attraction between them was evident. Corrie ten Boom, the Dutch woman who lived through the nightmare of the Holocaust in Europe, later wrote, "Forgiveness is an act of the will, and the will can function regardless of the temperature of the heart."

While it may be difficult to forgive our spouse, it is ultimately something we choose to do whether we feel like doing it or not. It is an act of our will, and our will can function regardless of how warm or cold our heart may be. We need to realize that the human heart was never designed for bitterness, only for love. We must get rid of the resentment, anger, and desire for revenge if we are ever to know true intimacy and heart connection in marriage.

Healing

This brings us to the next step in softening our hearts: *We must let Jesus disconnect the pain of past hurts in our heart.*

One of the great figures of the Old Testament is a man named Joseph. As a seventeen-year-old boy, he was stripped, thrown into a pit to die, and ultimately sold into slavery. And this unspeakable pain was inflicted on his young heart by his very own brothers.

Joseph would spend the next thirteen years as a slave in a foreign country. Though he served his master with faithfulness and integrity, he was falsely accused by his owner's wife of a serious crime he did not commit. He was thrown into prison without trial and left to languish for years on end.

Am I in the Place of God?

Yet the God he served did not forget Joseph. When the time was right, he was elevated to the second highest position in all of Egypt. He became the man who saved literally millions from death by starvation, including his own treacherous brothers, who assumed he was dead and gone forever. Later, when his brothers came and bowed before him and begged his forgiveness (assuming he would exact his revenge given the right opportunity), he responded with some of the most astonishing words found in Scripture:

> But Joseph said to them, "Don't be afraid. Am I in the place of God? You intended to harm me, but God intended it for good to accomplish what is now being done, the saving of many lives. So then, don't be afraid. I will provide for you and your children." And he reassured them and spoke kindly to them (Genesis 50:19-21).

The Ministry of Jesus to the Hurting Heart

One of the great works of God in our lives is to disconnect the pain of our past hurts and traumas and replace it with His peace and kindness. Jesus announced that the purpose of His earthly ministry was to do just that in the lives of those bruised and broken by life's hard experiences.

At the beginning of his three-year public ministry, Jesus returned to His hometown of Nazareth. He asked that He be given the scroll of the Scriptures and unrolled it until He found this passage from the prophet Isaiah (the event is recorded for us in Luke 4:16-21):

> "The Spirit of the Lord is on me,
>   because He has anointed me
>   to preach good news to the poor.
> He has sent me to proclaim freedom for
>   the prisoners

and recovery of sight to the blind,
to release the oppressed,
to proclaim the year of the Lord's favor."

If we continue reading in Isaiah 61, we find this additional ministry predicted of the coming Christ,

To comfort all who mourn,
and provide for those who grieve in Zion—
to bestow on them a crown of beauty
instead of ashes,
the oil of gladness
instead of mourning,
and a garment of praise
instead of a spirit of despair.
They will be called oaks of righteousness,
a planting of the LORD
for the display of His splendor.

(Isaiah 61:2-3)

Once we determine the painful events and episodes that have locked up a husband or wife's heart, then it's time to ask Jesus "to bestow on them a crown of beauty instead of ashes, the oil of gladness instead of mourning, and a garment of praise instead of a spirit of despair." In other words, we ask the living Christ to bring healing and release from all their pain and bring peace *to their hearts.*

What Did that Do to My Heart?

How does that work? It starts with the core conviction that Jesus hears and answers our heartfelt prayers. Jesus teaches us we can have this confidence in John 14:13-14, "And I will do whatever you ask in my name, so that the Son may bring glory to the Father. You may ask me for anything in my name, and I will do it."

A simple prayer such as the following is a good place to begin:

"Dear Jesus, when I was a young child I felt such intense rejection (or whatever your core issue is) from my family, particularly my brothers and sisters. What did that rejection do to my heart? How would You heal my heart?"

Whenever we ask God to speak to us, His answer will be consistent with the Scriptures. Perhaps He'll bring to mind biblical passages such as, "Fear not, for I have redeemed you; I have summoned you by name; you are mine" (Isaiah 43:1), and "The LORD himself goes before you and will be with you; he will never leave you nor forsake you. Do not be afraid; do not be discouraged" (Deuteronomy 31:8).

The important principle is to bring people to Jesus in prayer. He will minister to the heart of the hurting person. If it is healing of rejection, God will do so by assuring us of His unconditional love and acceptance. The apostle John tells us, "Yet to all who received [Jesus], to those who believed in his name, he gave the right to become children of God, children born not of natural descent, nor of a human decision or a husband's will, but born of God" (John 1:12-13).

Jesus Was There that Terrible Night

Another young husband was struggling with fear and anxiety that controlled his life. As we prayed for God to show him the cause of this disabling fear, an auto accident he was in as a child came to mind. He vividly remembered the cold and dark winter's night when a car slid across the ice and slammed into the car door next to where he was seated. It shattered the glass, and his mother screamed hysterically. While he was praying he started to shake.

"Ask Jesus where He was the night you were hit," I (Bob) encouraged him.

"Jesus, where were You the night the car hit me?" he prayed.

We waited a moment, then suddenly the young man looked up with astonishment in his eyes. "Jesus was standing between the car and my door—that's why I'm still alive." He broke down and wept at the thought that God had actually spared his life that night. At that moment a dam in his heart seemed to burst open. "God has been with me every minute of my life hasn't He?" he said with overflowing gratitude and joy.

"Indeed He has," I replied.

The psalmist David says that God's presence is the one constant in our lives,

> Where can I go from your Spirit?
>   Where can I flee from your presence?
> If I go up to the heavens, you are there;
>   if I make my bed in the depths, you are there.
> If I rise on the wings of the dawn,
>   if I settle on the far side of the sea,
> even there your hand will guide me;
>   your right hand will hold me fast.
> If I say, "Surely the darkness will hide me
>   and the light become night around me,"
> even the darkness will not be dark to you;
>   the night will shine like the day,
>   for darkness is as light to you…
> All the days ordained for me
>   were written in your book
>   before one of them came to be.
> How precious to me are your thoughts, O God!
>   How vast is the sum of them!
>
> (Psalm 139:7-12,16-17)

This young husband realized that not even a terrifying car accident could separate him from the love of God in Christ Jesus.

One of the interesting by-products of his heart release from fear and anxiety was his newfound love for God. Though he had been a Christian for years, he now experienced a new connection with Christ.

"When I realized that Jesus had been with me each and every day of my life, a new love for Christ entered my heart," he said later. "I've been a believer for most of my life. But now I can't think about my Friend and Savior Jesus without smiling. I love Him much more than I ever have before."

Once he was free from his crippling fear and worry, he was able to open his heart to his wife and children in a new way. Others soon noticed the joy in his countenance. God had indeed given him "a garment of praise instead of a spirit of despair."

Let Not Your Hearts Be Troubled

Can we trust that God will speak peace to our hearts when we approach Him through Christ? Can we bring our worst pain and heartaches to Him and find help and comfort? Listen to these words of Jesus,

> "Do not let your hearts be troubled. Trust in God; trust also in me…All this I have spoken while still with you. But the Counselor, the Holy Spirit, whom the Father will send in my name, will teach you all things and will remind you of everything I have said to you. Peace I leave with you; my peace I give to you. I do not give to you as the world gives. Do not let your hearts be troubled and do not be afraid" (John 14:1,25-27).

Connection

The fourth and final step in this healing process is this: *Connect with your spouse on an intimate heart-to-heart level.*

Remember what Jesus said was the primary cause of the breakup of marriages? In Matthew 19:8 He teaches us, "Moses permitted you to divorce because your hearts were hard. But it was not this way from the beginning." If hard hearts are the main reason couples can't connect with each other, then softened hearts will have the opposite effect. Instead of living with a disabling *heart attack,* the couple will experience a new and powerful *heart attract.*

Speak Directly to Your Spouse's Heart

Remember that the original design for marriage is oneness. As Genesis 2:24 instructs us, "For this reason a man will leave his father and mother and be united to his wife, and they will become one flesh." Later, in the last book of the Old Testament, God returns to this theme of oneness in marriage, "Has not the Lord made them one? In flesh and spirit they are His...So guard yourself in your spirit, and do not break faith with the wife of your youth" (Malachi 2:15).

This deep sense of oneness eludes many couples. They tend to operate on a day-to-day basis as two people sharing a common address, bank account, and bed. Other than that, they go about their lives connecting only at a head level to give and transact household business and information.

"What time will you be home?"

"After six."

"Should I save supper?"

"No, don't bother. I'll catch something on the way home."

Though such an exchange technically qualifies as communication, it falls far short of the goal of enjoying heart-to-heart intimacy and connection. To truly connect our hearts, we have to soften them toward the other person. We've seen that involves letting Christ take down the walls that pain and sin have constructed. It involves forgiving the people who have hurt us. It invites Christ to disconnect the pain of our past from our present so we are free to give and receive love.

This final step, though, requires that each spouse deliberately and intentionally speak regularly to the heart of their mate. It requires caring about the heart of the person we're married to with no expectations or preconditions. First Peter 1:22 tells us, "Now that you have purified yourselves by obeying the truth so that you have sincere love for your brothers, love one another deeply, from the heart." A few chapters later Peter returns to this same theme, "Above all, love each other deeply, because love covers over a multitude of sins" (4:8).

A practical way to love your spouse from the heart is to speak to their heart. At least ten minutes a day sit down and take their hands in yours, look lovingly into their eyes, and speak to their heart. Ask such questions as, "What troubles your heart today? What pain is there that you wish someone knew about? How could I care about that pain today?"

Experiencing a Deeper Intimacy in Marriage

While it may seem awkward at first, such heart-to-heart connection will soon become an important part of your lives. It's the one time that you can truly love each other from the heart and not just the head.

Such a deep heart connection will break down walls of hurt, loneliness, and misunderstanding between you. It will lift your spirit and comfort your inner heart. Once you begin to experience the power and attraction of caring for each other's heart, it will begin to change your entire relationship.

Geoffrey and Sara were having serious problems. Geoffrey struggled with abandonment issues, and Sara was given to serious bouts of depression. The mutual pain they inflicted on each other had reached a breaking point.

As they sat in my (Bob's) office, I encouraged them to turn and look at each other. They both fidgeted in their seats as they slowly adjusted their chairs to face each other.

"Now take each other's hands and look one another in the eye," I said.

"This feels strange," Geoffrey said.

"That may be true, but don't you want to experience intimacy on a much deeper level? You need an emotional connection between the two of you. That's what your hearts have been longing for."

They each took a deep breath and made eye contact for a moment, then glanced away. No question about it, this was really awkward. Ultimately, they summoned the needed courage and made tentative eye contact.

"Sara," I said, "would you ask Geoffrey if there is a little boy's heart inside him that has always wanted to feel loved?"

"Geoffrey, is there the heart of a little boy inside that's always wanted to feel loved?" she asked.

This was no small question for Geoffrey. His father had died while he was young and living in England. His mother later abandoned him, and her relatives raised him. All this before he was five. Geoffrey spent much of his formative years alone and unsupervised—essentially a street child in London.

The only difference between him and a figure from a Charles Dickens novel was that he had a family to come home to at night. His custodial grandparents did their best, but they simply didn't know how to connect on a heart level. He grew up with an abandoned heart that eventually led him to develop an immoral heart to cover the pain.

Though Geoffrey was taken in by caring Christian foster parents in Scotland during his teenage years, the awful damage of abandonment and rejection was already done. Deep lines of sorrow, rejection, and anger were etched on his face.

I coached his wife to repeat after me, "Does that little boy wish he had been raised with a father?" Slowly she repeated the statement, and incredibly her husband's face began to soften.

"Yes," he said quietly. "I always wished I had a father."

"Little boys aren't meant to be left all alone all day without a daddy or mommy, are they?" Again his wife looked into his face and repeated the probing question.

Again his voice softened. "No, they are not."

"What if I loved the heart of that little abandoned boy, would you mind that?" She repeated the question to her husband.

"No, I wouldn't mind that," he mumbled.

"What if I made my heart a safe place for that little boy's heart to come to?"

"I would like that—very much."

Tears began to form in both their eyes. The initial awkwardness started to diminish as their hearts began to soften toward each other.

A Sacred Moment

"Now it's your turn, Geoffrey," I said. "Turn to your wife and ask if there is the heart of a little girl hurting and wanting to be loved."

He repeated my words and she nodded.

"Ask her if that little girl's heart has felt rejected her entire life."

"Yes, it has," she said.

"What if I loved that little girl's heart and protected it, would that be okay?"

A new kindness appeared in his voice, one that seemed to draw the two of them closer to each other. After several minutes of such intimate heart-to-heart dialogue, the two were locked in a loving gaze toward each other.

"Geoffrey, tell her that you are deeply sorry for hurting her heart," I said.

It was amazing to witness what happened next. While Geoffrey had started our time together defensive, evasive, and detached, he now couldn't take his eyes off his wife.

"I'm so sorry..." he said with new sincerity.

As Geoffrey and Sara looked into each other's soul through their mate's eyes, they saw something they had longed for but had been unable to find until now—the other person's heart.

The new connection between them became a sacred moment.

"Geoffrey, you've found your heart again, haven't you?" I said. "It's cracked open only a little bit, but the door is starting to open up, isn't it?"

He smiled. "Yes, it's starting to open up."

We closed our time together in prayer.

A Heart of Flesh for a Heart of Stone

This moment of heart-to-heart connection was only a beginning.

The two would have to continue this process if they were to save their marriage. But at least for this one evening they walked out of the room side by side. I even saw Geoffrey reach for Sara's hand as they walked toward their van.

What they experienced that day was the power of giving and receiving forgiveness combined with a genuine desire to care for the heart of their spouse. It was just a taste of the true intimacy God intends for each married couple. Once a couple tastes it, they will never forget it—nor will they ever want to.

When God does open heart surgery, the patients are never the same. He replaces their heart of stone with a heart of flesh—and a marriage is transformed.

> *Lord Jesus, I realize I need to forgive others if I'm to have a softened heart. I choose today to forgive other people, my family, and my spouse for the hurt they've caused me. I choose to release them from the moral debt they owe me. I agree to carry the emotional consequences of their hurtful actions by refusing to become bitter or demanding they pay the price for their actions. Show me again how much I have been forgiven by You, O Lord. Let me show that same grace and mercy to others, especially my spouse, whenever they offend me. Amen.*

Questions for You and Your Spouse to Discuss

1. Why does the idea of confession seem so unpleasant to you? How could confession and forgiveness change your marriage?

2. Why is it possible for two people to forgive even if they don't feel like it? Why is it necessary to pay the emotional price in order to forgive?

3. How can Jesus disconnect the emotional pain in your

lives? What experiences do you wish Jesus would heal in your life?

4. Why is it so much easier to communicate on an intellectual level rather than heart to heart? Has anyone ever actually cared for your heart? Would you mind if that someone who cared was your spouse?

CHAPTER 6

How to Know My Heart Is Softened

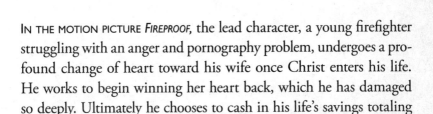

IN THE MOTION PICTURE *FIREPROOF*, the lead character, a young firefighter struggling with an anger and pornography problem, undergoes a profound change of heart toward his wife once Christ enters his life. He works to begin winning her heart back, which he has damaged so deeply. Ultimately he chooses to cash in his life's savings totaling $24,000 to purchase his ailing mother-in-law a much-needed wheelchair and hospital bed.

It is then that his wife's heart begins to soften toward him. Where she was once consumed with bitterness and entangled in an emotional affair at work, she now is desperate to seek out her husband and ask his forgiveness. As the film so dramatically portrays, when two hard hearts are softened, they become childlike hearts once again. Both partners demonstrate a new innocence, trust, obedience, love, humility, and willingness to forgive each other. As a result, a new marriage is born in the ashes of the old one.

THE ASSURANCE OF REAL CHANGE

A softened heart can fundamentally alter the nature of your marriage relationship. For some, your change of heart will be dramatic and immediate. For others, it will be far more subtle and occur over a longer period of time. Either way, you will begin to discover the intimacy and connection God designed for your marriage.

How can we know that our heart has softened (or is softening) toward our spouse? How can we be sure what's happening in our marriage is more than a transient emotional experience? Just as important, how can we avoid returning to the old hard-hearted patterns of the past?

Scripture points out at least five (there are certainly more) distinct evidences of a softened heart. Let's look at each one and see how they can give us assurance that something deep, fundamental, and lasting is taking place in our heart and marriage.

Childlike

Test Number One: Our heart is softened if it is now a more child-like heart.

Let's review what we've learned about childlike hearts. The heart of a child is naturally innocent, trusting, obedient, loving, humble, and forgiving. While we are all born with a fallen and sinful nature, the tenderness of a young child's heart is clearly evident as Jesus pointed out in Matthew 19, "for the kingdom of heaven belongs to such as these."

For the most part, childlike innocence means children are not drawn to evil but repelled by it. Guileless, they naturally believe in the good intentions and loving motives of the people closest to them. Childlike love moves them to care for those around them without expecting something in return. Childlike humility means they often treat others as more important than themselves. Finally, and perhaps the most remarkable of all their characteristics, childlike forgiveness releases others from the debt owed them as soon as they are asked for it (and often before).

Jesus said such childlike traits are typical of the heart characteristics of those who have entered God's eternal kingdom. While we are saved by the grace of God alone and not by works, the presence of these traits is evidence that a dramatic spiritual change has taken place in our hearts. (By the way, the greatest percentage of Christians became believers when they were under the age of eighteen.)

One couple that had been through a bitter season in their marriage chose to soften their hearts toward each other. To display the joy forgiveness had brought to her now childlike heart, the wife decorated the oak coatrack in their hallway with yellow ribbons. When her husband came home, he found it standing inside the front door with a note taped to it, "Who cares if it's not a real oak tree? Any old oak will do when you're in love."

Beautiful Attitudes

Test Number Two: Our heart is softened if it displays beautiful attitudes.

The essence of a changed heart toward God is found in the Sermon on the Mount. Let's review these beautiful attitudes as Jesus taught them:

> "Blessed are the poor in spirit,
>   for theirs is the kingdom of heaven.
> Blessed are those who mourn,
>   for they will be comforted.
> Blessed are the meek,
>   for they will inherit the earth.
> Blessed are those who hunger and thirst for
>   righteousness,
>   for they will be filled.
> Blessed are the merciful,
>   for they will be shown mercy.
> Blessed are the pure in heart,
>   for they will see God.

Blessed are the peacemakers,
for they will be called sons of God.
Blessed are those who are persecuted because of
righteousness,
for theirs is the kingdom of heaven.

Blessed are you when people insult you, persecute you and
falsely say all kinds of evil against you because of me. Rejoice
and be glad, because great is your reward in heaven, for
in the same way they persecuted the prophets who were
before you" (Matthew 5:1-12).

Everyday Beautiful Attitudes

Applied to marriage these beatitudes (or beautiful attitudes) exemplify a new and tender heart toward God. When applied to marriage, these attitudes are lived out this way, "I find my life is poor without you, I long to share your sorrows, I promise to use my strength to help rather than control you, I desire to treat you in a right way, I will quickly show you mercy when offended, I will look for God's face and glory in our sexual purity, I will take the initiative to make peace when it's disrupted, I am willing even to suffer to do the right thing toward you, and I'm committed to rejoicing even when I'm misunderstood by you."

A softened heart is a transformed heart. We can have our hearts changed by Christ to such an extent that our inclination is no longer toward what is evil and sad but toward what is good and beautiful. Our new heart, filled with God's Spirit, naturally produces beautiful attitudes, which in turn produce a beautiful marriage relationship.

One well-known marriage author described for his radio audience the ordeal of his wife's open-heart surgery. Though married for decades, when the surgeon emerged in his green scrubs to announce his wife came through just fine, he told his listeners he broke down and cried like a baby. His tears of gratitude were driven by the heartfelt attitude that his life would be so much poorer without her. Losing her was beyond his imagination. Such a beautiful attitude is symptomatic of a softened heart.

Exclusive

Test Number Three: Our heart is softened if it is attracted only to our spouse.

The process of leaving, uniting, and becoming one flesh implies an exclusive relationship. It allows no room for competitors or substitutes. It results in two hearts so attracted to each other that we cannot imagine sharing our physical and emotional married love with someone else. We find each other more than enough—our love is satisfying, desirable, and sufficient. Distracting thoughts, nagging urges, and emotional attractions simply have no lasting place because our heart is drawn to one person and one person only—our spouse. In short, a softened heart is free, faithful, and fulfilled.

The actor Paul Newman was once asked how he resisted temptation playing opposite beautiful and alluring leading ladies. His answer was simple: "Why should I settle for hamburger at work when I can have steak at home?" (I say pass the A-1 and Heinz 57!) By the way, he enjoyed the banquet at home for over fifty years before his death to cancer.

This is not to say we will never experience temptation. None of us is immune to the devil's assaults on our thought life. However, with our softened hearts toward God and our spouse, we have in place a sure and steady defense. Combined with our faith, it renders "flaming arrows" harmless and ineffective. When we consider the immense satisfaction and fulfillment our sexual relationship brings us within our marriage, the thought of straying seems so entirely unnecessary if not absurd.

Never Call Temptation Love

Let us say a word to anyone who struggles with an intense temptation to stray from your vows. First, please realize that it isn't love drawing you to the other person. It is illicit desire acting as an emotional anesthetic, which promises to deaden the pain in your heart.

Can we say this in the strongest and plainest terms possible? *The strong attraction you feel to the other person is not from God.*

What is tempting you is the world, the flesh, the devil, or all three at once. The Bible says those three are at war with the Spirit of God that lives within you, "So I say, live by the Spirit, and you will not gratify the desires of the sinful nature. For the sinful nature desires what is contrary to the Spirit, and the Spirit what is contrary to the sinful nature. They are in conflict with each other, so that you do not do what you want" (Galatians 5:16-17).

The war going on inside is a real conflict. It isn't a harmless emotional struggle simply between the good and the best, boredom and excitement, or Option A or Option B. It's an all-out, winner-take-all-loser-is-destroyed war between good and evil, blessing and destruction, and ultimately life and death. Proverbs 5:3-5 lays it on the table,

> For the lips of an adulteress drip honey,
>   and her speech is smoother than oil;
> but in the end she is bitter as gall,
>   sharp as a double-edged sword.
> Her feet go down to death;
>   her steps lead straight to the grave.

Seven Strategies to Defeat Sexual Temptation

It is vital that you win this battle. The future of your marriage, the well-being of your children, and your spiritual integrity depend on it. Recognizing the seriousness of the struggle you are facing, let us offer a few simple steps to deal with temptation when it strikes:

1. What to say to the devil. If the devil whispers in your ear, "Isn't she [or he] hot?" simply respond by saying, "Yes, and so is hell." Remember, the devil hates you and hates God and wants only your complete destruction, not your happiness and fulfillment.

2. The wallet shield. When tempted by someone else, immediately take out a wallet picture of your wife (husband) and children. Look at their faces carefully and then imagine the conversation you will inevitably need to have one day if you violate your marriage vows. Remember, these are the precious handful of people on earth who have trusted you the most. Try to imagine packing the things you own in your car and pulling out of the driveway while your youngest child chases after you screaming, "Daddy (Mommy), please don't leave! When are you coming home again? Please don't go." You'll have to respond, "I'm sorry, but Mommy and Daddy can't live together anymore. I can't explain it all to you—but someday you'll understand." If you knew such an intensely sad and agonizing moment awaits you, wouldn't it pop the powerful fantasy you're toying with right now?

3. Think clearly. Ask yourself, "If the person I'm drawn to is willing to cheat on their spouse in order to have me, what's to keep them from cheating on me in the future if they meet someone more attractive?"

4. Remember the return of Christ. When I stand someday in the presence of Jesus Christ (which we all will) and look Him in the eye, will He accept whatever excuse I'm using at the moment to be unfaithful to my spouse?

5. Repeat this to yourself. When tempted by someone, say to yourself, *She (or he) cannot complete me. Only Jesus can fill every empty place in my heart.* After you've traded away your spiritual integrity and sexual purity, will you be more or less a person than you were before?

6. Run, don't walk. The Bible tells us to run and not to look back when faced with sexual temptation. Don't slow down until the other person is literally out of reach. Make whatever immediate (and even drastic) changes are needed to your schedule, friendships, job situations, social circles, and Internet access to unplug the temptation. Then do more than seems necessary to put safeguards between you and the person you're tempted to pursue (or are being pursued by). No sacrifice is too great right now to protect and save your marriage from ruin.

7. Examine the hole in your heart. Ask the Holy Spirit to show you the damaged portion of your heart that gives the world, the flesh, and the devil the opportunity they've been waiting for. Once you see the real cause of your longing for someone other than your spouse, you'll discover it has nothing to do with genuine love, fulfilling sexual experiences, or emotionally intimate relationships. Instead it has to do only with the devil offering to meet a legitimate need in your life in an illegitimate way. Recognize the false intimacy he's offering you, and don't allow him to rent any space in your head.

A friend of ours told of being in a hotel elevator on a business trip far out of state. As the doors opened two attractive women approached him in a provocative way and said, "Do you like pretty girls?" Without hesitation he replied, "Yes, and I'm married to one back home." The two women turned away before the elevator doors closed.

Remember, we know our heart is softened when we are attracted only to our spouse. Yes, temptation may come, but it is quickly recognized as "hamburger" rather than the "steak" awaiting you at home.

Sacrificing

Test Number Four: Our heart is softened if we sacrificially love our wife or lovingly honor our husband.

When our hearts are hard as husbands, we find it difficult to give up any of our wants or desires for the sake of our wives. We view their needs as an inconvenience if not a downright nuisance.

When our hearts are hard as wives, we likely view our husbands as consistent failures in many areas of life, including our marriage relationship. We have no intention of showing them honor or admiration until the changes we want take place. The idea of respecting them seems ridiculous if not hypocritical.

However, when our hearts are softened, we see sacrificing for our wife as a welcome opportunity and honoring our husband as a true privilege.

Let's return for a moment to the day we stood before the minister and recited our marriage vows. Chances are we truly meant what we were saying (at least as much as it was possible to understand their true meaning).

Let's Review What You Promised

What unconditional vows to love your wife did you make? What unconditional promise to respect your husband did you make? If you used the traditional marriage vows, let me refresh your memory. And even if you didn't use traditional vows, I suspect the vows you recited included many of the same elements.

> Will you have this (woman/man) to be your wedded (wife/ husband), to live together in the holy estate of matrimony? Will you love (her/him), comfort (her/him), honor and keep (her/him), in sickness and in health; and forsaking all others keep yourself only unto (her/him) so long as you both shall live?
>
> I take you to be my wedded (wife/husband), to have and to hold, from this day forward, for better, for worse, for richer, for poorer, in sickness and in health, to love and to cherish, till death us do part, according to God's holy ordinance; and thereto I pledge you my faith.

Do you notice the lack of any qualifying clauses in those promises? We didn't say, "I will love, comfort, honor, and keep you if you earn it...if you are the husband you should be to me...if you are the wife I really deserve...if you meet my emotional needs...if you meet my physical needs."

No, the day we married we made promises independent of our mate's worthiness, performance, or ability to reciprocate. We pledged, "I will do the right and loving things because they are the right and loving things to do. Even if you should fail to fully keep your end of the bargain, I will continue to keep my end because I have promised to do so."

Keeping Your Vows Even When It Hurts

We have met spouses who still live by their original vows even though their husband or wife has openly chosen to break their marriage covenant. Are they fools for choosing to remain true to what they promised? We don't think so. Rather they are simply keeping their word and the promises they made before God.

Consider the great reward Scripture promises for those who remain righteous even when those around them do not:

> Lord, who may dwell in your sanctuary?
>> Who may live on your holy hill?
> He whose walk is blameless
>> and who does what is righteous,
>> who speaks the truth from his heart
> and has no slander on his tongue,
>> who does his neighbor no wrong...
>> who keeps his oath
>> even when it hurts...
> He who does these things
>> will never be shaken.
>
> (Psalm 15:1-5)

When our hearts are softened toward each other, we "keep our oath" in marriage "even when it hurts." But isn't that a formula for being taken advantage of by an unprincipled or dishonest spouse?

Let's be clear. We're not suggesting we deny what our spouse is doing if they are violating the marriage vows. We're not suggesting you put yourself in harm's way if your spouse is acting violently or with cruelty toward you or the children. Nor are we saying there is never a time or place to recognize the marriage covenant has been consistently violated and the marriage has ended.

When the Storm Is Over

What we are saying is that keeping our vows until the marriage is formally ended, regardless of the other person's behavior, brings with it special rewards only the righteous can enjoy. For example, it is never the right thing to do to return adultery for adultery. The Bible promises those who continue to live righteous lives despite the trial their spouse is putting them through will enjoy a special intimacy and closeness with God. The foundation of our life will remain secure. Proverbs 10:25 promises us,

> When the storm has swept by, the wicked are gone,
>   but the righteous stand firm forever.

Ultimately we are accountable for keeping the pledges we made to God Himself on our wedding day. While we cannot control our spouse's behavior, we can continue to display a loving, respectful, and kind heart toward the person we married. Keeping such promises in a loving and righteous way toward our spouse is living and convincing proof that our hearts are softened.

We know one couple that enjoyed several years of active ministry. Yet due to an accidental drug overdose during a hospitalization, the husband's body was ruined beyond repair. It left him housebound and hardly able to walk or stand. Yet his loving and faithful wife remains close to him. She cares for his daily hygienic needs and other duties usually reserved for medical staff. Her softened heart gives her the strength and desire to honor him even in his disabled condition. She is keeping her vows even when it hurts. We believe a great reward awaits her both now and in the life to come.

We also respect those spouses who keep their vows even when they are the victim of an unwanted divorce.

Soft Toward God

Test Number Five: Our heart is softened if it is softened toward God.

There is a biblical order to the reconciliation of relationships. It begins with being reconciled to God first and foremost. This occurs when we accept Jesus Christ and His offer of salvation. It continues as we allow Him to make our heart like His heart as we grow in grace and knowledge. Then, as a result of our reconciliation with God, we are reconciled with others, starting with those closest to us. That means reconciliation with our spouse if we are married. As the following story illustrates, God works in this wonderful and established order to bring healing and reconciliation into our lives.

Revival in the Bluegrass Country

Asbury College was a little known Southern liberal arts school through much of its history. The town of Wilmore is a small and somewhat isolated village in the rolling bluegrass hills of central Kentucky. The town was established in the 1800s, built in the days of Daniel Boone's nephew. But apart from the thoroughbred horses raised on nearby farms, the town has been all but ignored.

But as Robert Coleman recounts in his book, *One Divine Moment: The Asbury Revival,* all that was about to change. During a routine morning chapel service in Hughes Auditorium in February 1970, a college senior stood at the microphone and stunned his classmates by confessing,

> "I'm not believing that I'm standing here telling you what God has done for me. I've wasted my time in college up to now. But Christ has met me, and I'm different. Last night the Holy Spirit flooded in and filled my life. Now for the first time ever, I am excited about being a Christian. I wouldn't want to go back to the emptiness of yesterday for anything."

A college professor, sensing the convicting presence of God's Spirit, walked up to the platform and invited any other students who wanted to pray to come forward to the altar. One eyewitness recounts what happened next—events that would change the course of an entire generation:

No sooner had the invitation been extended than a mass of students moved forward...There was not room for all who wanted to pray at the altar. Many had to kneel in the front seats of the auditorium. Their prayers were mingled with heartfelt contrition and outbursts of joy. It was evident that God was moving upon His people in power. The presence of the Lord was so real that all other interests seemed unimportant. The bell sounded for classes to begin, but it went unheeded.

Relationships Healed and Sins Confessed

This was only the beginning. As the day wore on, more and more students lined up at the front of the auditorium.

> Those who had come to the altar—after a time of prayer—rose, joining those on the platform and with tears, made confessions. These acknowledgments ranged from cheating and theft to having animosity, prejudice and jealousy. Some made their way to individuals in the congregation to ask forgiveness and to make restitution. Old enmities were melted with the fervent love of God...Students in all classes, from freshmen to seniors, poured out their souls, asking forgiveness and exhorting others to heed the call of God. As the confessions were made, other students streamed to the front, filling the altar and the front seats.

For six remarkable days the Holy Spirit continued to wash across this small Southern campus. He was changing lives, healing relationships, and renewing the students' love for Christ. The unexpected arrival of the nearness of God did not end at the doors to the chapel, however. It soon began to spread across the nation. Newspapers, wire services, and local television stations arrived on campus to chronicle the amazing events unfolding before their eyes.

Students' hearts were so affected by God that they began to organize into groups to take their newfound love for Christ across the country. The power of what was happening at Asbury began to have results in a much larger circle of influence.

We were both affected by the revival stirring. Students came from Asbury up to Bob's home church in Minneapolis. Bob was a high school freshman, and his heart was moved when the visiting students challenged the audience to give their whole lives for the gospel. Cheryl was an eighth grader when a different group of Asbury students came to her father's church in Flint, Michigan, to share how Christ was moving to revolutionize the college and seminary campus in Kentucky. They also rented a large auditorium in downtown Flint, and it was filled with people and the presence of the Holy Spirit as God used them to win hundreds to the Lord.

Love Comes to a Gas Station

One group of students stopped at a gas station in Georgia to fill their tank. However, they had lost the gas credit card they needed, so they went to another filling station close by. It was owned and operated by a young couple that had been married less than a year. One of the college girls started a conversation with the wife, who confessed that her love for her husband had turned out to be nothing more than infatuation. She was thinking of calling it quits on their new marriage.

> [The wife explained] she was miserable, empty, disillusioned and about to leave her husband, whose deep love for her she could not reciprocate. After witnessing to her of Christ and His love, the student asked the girl if she did not want to accept Christ, who could fill her with perfect love and free her from her sin and self. The young woman bowed her head and uttered a fervent prayer of confession and asked the Lord to come into her life and cleanse her. "I feel so clean! So clean!" she exclaimed. Then she prayed for God to take away her unwillingness to love her husband.

While the two girls talked, one of the fellows witnessed to the husband between customers. After his wife told him of her experience with Christ and of the love He had given her for him, the young man also received Christ. Three and a half hours after stopping for gas the witness team left two happy young people united through Christ to each other in a genuine love. Revival had come to a Georgia garage.

Notice what happened—the couple softened their heart first toward Christ and then toward each other.

Conclusion

Thank God we can know that our hearts are softened toward our spouse. We will possess the precious characteristics of a childlike heart in our interactions, we will display beautiful attitudes in our daily life, we will be attracted only to our partner despite temptation, we will welcome the opportunity to show love and respect even when it's difficult, and we will live in the joy and power of a revived heart tender toward Christ and our spouse.

Doesn't that sound inviting?

> *Lord Jesus, I ask You to give me a childlike heart toward my spouse. Restore in me a heart of kindness, innocence, trust, humility, and willingness to forgive. Replace any harsh or prideful thoughts with words of thanksgiving and gratitude for my mate. Give me the wisdom to resist and run from any temptation that would compromise my marriage vows. Build hedges around our marriage that will protect us from moral compromise or sin. Let me daily demonstrate sacrificial love toward my spouse and love them as Christ loves the church. Do a new work in my heart, O Lord. Revive my heart and give me the love I had at first for my spouse, and for You, O Lord. Then I will know my heart has truly softened. Amen.*

Questions for You and Your Spouse to Discuss

1. Why is it important to know for certain that you have softened your heart toward your mate? Does God want you to have that assurance?

2. What beautiful attitudes do you see at work in each other? Which attitudes do you long to see developed more?

3. Why is it vital that you have a strategy to defeat sexual temptation when it strikes? What is the devil's goal for your marriage? What is Christ's goal for you?

4. What brings about true revival in a marriage? Should you begin to pray for that?

CHAPTER 7

If Only One Heart Softens

JASON COULD NOT QUIT SMILING at the end of the weekend marriage conference. A twenty-eight-year-old medical student, he had gone through the process of allowing Christ to disconnect his pain and forgiving those who had hurt him. His face reflected a joy he could hardly contain. Next to him sat his wife, Diana, a registered nurse who seemed tense and disengaged from the process. While Jason had responded enthusiastically to the invitation to soften his heart, Diana mainly went through the motions. The two went back to their medical school apartment still in very different places in their spiritual lives.

Two years earlier they had met and fallen in love at the hospital where Diana was a cardiac nurse and Jason was just finishing a medical internship. Neither were believers the year they met, but they had much in common and enjoyed each other's company. They got married twelve months later and settled into the residency Jason had secured at the same hospital. The next summer Jason was invited by a fellow student to join him on a fishing trip sponsored by a Christian camp. On that trip, Jason first heard the gospel and accepted Christ as his Savior.

A House Divided

Jason returned home brimming with enthusiasm for his newfound faith. Diana listened politely but explained she was not ready for that step. From that time onward, they were spiritually mismatched in their marriage. Whenever Jason suggested they go to church, Diana balked. Whenever Jason tried to read the Bible to her, she would find something she needed to do in the apartment. Whenever he suggested they pray, she would ask him to please not pressure her to become a Christian.

The two were drifting further and further apart when Jason suggested they attend a marriage conference at Jason's home church. At the conference, the speaker explained the steps to softening your heart, and Jason responded to the invitation to do so. He could hardly contain the newfound freedom and joy he felt that evening as much of his past pain was beginning to be resolved.

Not so for Diana. She went home more convinced than ever she could not forgive those who had hurt her—and she definitely wasn't interested in prayer.

The Weber Grill Principle of Marriage

What happens when only one spouse softens their heart? Is the marriage lost? Is it game over?

The Marriage Miracle is designed to work with two softened hearts, not just one. If one spouse refuses to cooperate, the couple will not be able to resolve their issues, at least for now. This is true regardless of how much time, effort, or counseling is invested in their relationship. Jesus said the ultimate cause of divorce (and all other marriage ills) is a hardened heart. Until the heart issue is dealt with, all other attempts at healing the marriage will be temporary and superficial at best. As the writer of Proverbs tells us,

> Like a coating of glaze over earthenware
> are fervent lips with an evil heart.

> A malicious man [or woman] disguises himself
> with his lips,
> but in his heart he harbors deceit.

> (Proverbs 26:23-24)

Regardless of what we might say with our lips (even in marriage counseling), what is in our hearts will ultimately prevail.

But with that said, *never underestimate the power of one softened heart to influence the other heart.* While there is no guarantee one softened heart will call out a softened heart in the other spouse, it remains the best opportunity to see it happen. We call this "The Weber Grill Principle of Marriage." Weber grills were first produced in our fair city of Chicago, and now several popular restaurants exist by that same name. Sizzling and savory food is prepared over real charcoal embers in a barrel-like stove; to walk in the door is to catch the sumptuous scent of a summer backyard barbeque in progress.

What is the Weber Grill Principle of Marriage? It's described by Solomon in Proverbs,

> If your enemy is hungry, give him food to eat;
> if he is thirsty, give him water to drink.
> In doing this, you will heap burning coals
> on his head,
> and the Lord will reward you.

> (25:21-22)

This same passage is repeated and expanded in the New Testament,

> Do not repay anyone evil for evil. Be careful to do what is right in the eyes of everybody. If it is possible, so far as it depends on you, live at peace with everyone. Do not take revenge, my friends, but leave room for God's wrath, for it is written, "It is mine to avenge; I will repay," says the Lord. On the contrary:

"If your enemy is hungry, feed him;
   if he is thirsty, give him something to drink.
In doing this, you will heap burning coals on his
      head."
Do not be overcome by evil, but overcome evil with
good (Romans 12:17-21).

Dealing with a Desire for Payback

It's possible at this moment that your enemy is none other than your husband or wife. In their hard-hearted state, they may have said or done things to irritate, hurt, or even devastate you. Perhaps you feel the temptation to pay them back for the wrongs they have done to you. Perhaps you're even considering walking away from the marriage.

The Bible says it's precisely at such a moment that we are to soften our heart. We need to allow compassion and forgiveness to take over our words and actions. Rather than giving in to our sinful impulses or allowing hostility to build, we are to live at peace with everyone. We are to leave retribution and revenge in the hands of a holy God. Our calling is to reach out to our hard-hearted spouse with acts of unmerited grace and kindness. We are to do the equivalent of offering them food and drink if they were hungry and thirsty.

Why does God command us to do the very opposite of what our sinful human nature screams for us to do in payback to our hard-hearted spouse? The Bible's answer is simple: "In doing this you will heap burning coals on his head." That's the Weber Grill Principle of Marriage.

As we show our spouse unmerited kindness and love, it's as if a red-hot Weber grill filled with glowing charcoal briquettes is dumped out on our spouse's head. While that sounds mean-spirited if not downright vengeful, it actually symbolizes the power of kindness to bring searing conviction to an otherwise stubborn and calloused heart. It's another way of saying our acts of unexpected mercy, grace, and compassion can have a dramatic impact on our spouse's hardened heart. It may ultimately lead them to contrition and repentance.

Jesus teaches a similar radical love for others who have caused us pain: "You have heard that it was said, 'Eye for eye, and tooth for tooth.' But I tell you, Do not resist an evil person. If someone strikes you on the right cheek, turn to him the other also" (Matthew 5:38).

Maintaining Boundaries and a Soft Heart Go Together

This means in a marriage a softened heart will not return insult for insult, argument for argument, or wrong for wrong. Rather it will resort to trusting in the power of love, forgiveness, and patience to do its good work in our hard-hearted spouse. A softened heart will maintain healthy boundaries in marriage and not permit abuse or infidelity to occur in any form, and it will continue to show love even if that love is not reciprocated. A softened heart finds its strength in the heart of God. It clings to the belief that Christ is still at work in their mate's heart even if there is no immediate or tangible evidence.

If you feel returning love in the face of insults and provocation is too much to ask of you, remember that God showed us this same unmerited love and kindness when we were still unbelievers. Paul reminds us, "Or do you show contempt for the riches of his kindness, tolerance and patience, not realizing that God's kindness leads you toward repentance?" (Romans 2:4).

It bears repeating that while a soft heart needs to remain soft, no spouse should remain in a seriously abusive environment. If you find yourself in such a situation, you need to seek adequate protection and outside support while seeking to reconcile with your mate. That means it may be necessary to separate for a season and even bring in the authorities to provide protection and accountability. There is no contradiction between drawing firm boundaries of behavior in marriage and maintaining a softened heart.

The ultimate example of retaining a softened heart in the face of wrongdoing is Christ on the cross. While hanging in agony Jesus prayed for His persecutors, "'Father, forgive them, for they do not know what they are doing.' And they divided up his clothes by casting lots. The people stood watching, and the rulers even sneered at him. They said, 'He saved others; let him save himself if he is the Christ of God, the Chosen One'" (Luke 23:34-35).

Six Reasons to Keep Our Heart Soft

There are a number of compelling arguments for why we should maintain a soft heart even when our spouse's heart is as hard as cement.

1. A soft heart maintains an open and intimate relationship with God.

Even if our spouse is shutting us out of his or her life, by keeping a soft heart we can continue to enjoy uninterrupted fellowship with Jesus Christ. We can rely on a number of scriptural promises to keep us in close communion with God even when things are difficult. The Bible promises we can know Him in the fellowship of His sufferings (Philippians 3:10), when we draw near to God He will draw near to us (James 4:8), and even in distress we can know the peace that passes all understanding (Philippians 4:7).

On the other hand, if we choose to harden our heart, we will pay a great price in losing much of our fellowship and intimacy with God. First John 4:20-21 explains, "If anyone says, 'I love God,' yet hates his brother, he is a liar. For anyone who does not love his brother, whom he has seen, cannot love God, whom he has not seen. And he has given us this command: Whoever loves God must also love his brother." Your brother in this case can mean your husband or wife. If we do not love the person we can see each day, the Bible says we do not love the God who remains unseen.

2. By keeping our hearts soft we can also discover spiritual lessons we would not otherwise learn.

Paul had an ongoing and painful difficulty that would not go away. It may have been a physical problem, such as poor eyesight or recurring pain from his numerous beatings and imprisonments. Or it may have been a relational issue, such as someone or a group of people who consistently opposed and persecuted him.

In any case, three times he prayed this "thorn in the flesh" would be taken from him. But Christ did not remove this thorn, whatever it was. Instead, Paul learned that God was teaching him a valuable spiritual lesson:

> But [Christ] said to me, "My grace is sufficient for you, for my power is made perfect in weakness." Therefore I will boast all the more gladly about my weaknesses, so that Christ's power may rest on me. That is why, for Christ's sake, I delight in weaknesses, in insults, in hardships, in persecutions, in difficulties. For when I am weak, then I am strong (2 Corinthians 12:9-10).

There are spiritual lessons for us to learn by keeping a softened heart when faced with a difficult spouse. We will learn that Christ's power is made perfect in our weakness and that His grace is sufficient for each day. Paul ended up saying he even "delighted" in weaknesses, insults, hardships, persecutions, and difficulties. Why? "For when I am weak, then I am strong."

3. A soft heart sets the right example for our children.

Children instinctively pick up on the tensions and problems between their parents. They can tell when one parent is not treating the other parent as they should.

On one occasion when our children were still quite young, we were driving in our van when Cheryl and I got into a small argument. I happened to be wearing a baseball cap with the words stitched on the back, "Men of Integrity." Apparently I was treating Cheryl in a less than loving fashion because right in the middle of our spat, a small voice came from the back seat, "Hey, Dad, what about men of integrity?"

It was like a rifle shot to my heart. My first instinct was to take that cap off and throw it out the window. My better instincts took over, so I turned and said, "Kids, are you saying I haven't been treating your mother right?"

"Yup," was the unanimous voice vote.

"Are you saying I need to apologize?"

"Yes," came a second chorus of little voices.

I knew I was had. So I turned to Cheryl and apologized right there on the spot. Then I turned and apologized to our four children for acting unkindly toward their mother.

It's vital to our children's well-being that we maintain a soft heart toward our spouse. That's true even when our life partner's heart may be brittle as steel against us. (It's also important for separated and divorced couples not to speak ill of each other in front of the children. Children's tender hearts were never designed to take sides with one parent against the other.) As parents, it's our solemn duty to model a softened heart toward our mate if we want our children to experience the security and love they desperately need. It furthermore sets an example for them to follow in their marriages when they grow up.

Even if just one spouse keeps their heart tender, it's enough to influence the children in the right direction. Tara was a single mother with three children. Her husband deserted her early in their marriage and married another woman. Yet Tara refused to speak ill of her ex-husband in front of the children. Hurt as she was by his betrayal, the well-being of her children came first. Today, all three children are married with families of their own and are solid believers in Jesus Christ.

While maintaining a soft heart is no guarantee your children will turn out right, it weights the process in the right direction. The psalmist David tells us,

> But from everlasting to everlasting
>   the LORD's love is with those who fear him,
>   and his righteousness with their children's children.
>
> (Psalm 103:17)

The writer of Proverbs adds further weight to this truth,

> He who fears the LORD has a secure fortress,
> and for his children it will be a refuge.
>
> (Proverbs 14:26)

4. A soft heart will open up your life to unexpected blessings.
Jesus made a bold and extravagant promise to those who resist the temptation to judge others (a judgmental heart is one form of a hardened heart):

> "Do not judge, and you will not be judged. Do not condemn, and you will not be condemned. Forgive, and you will be forgiven. Give, and it will be given to you. A good measure, pressed down, shaken together and running over, will be poured into your lap. For with the measure you use, it will be measured to you" (Luke 6:37-38).

As we measure out lavish amounts of kindness, tenderness, compassion, mercy, grace, and love toward a difficult spouse, this same generous and bountiful amount will be measured back to us. The reward may not come from the person we're married to, but God will see that the shipment of blessings is delivered to our door nonetheless.

5. A soft heart creates the best opportunity for our spouse's heart to change.
It may take weeks, months, or even years to see a softening occur in your mate's heart, but rest assured, not a moment or hour of kindness will have been wasted on your spouse in God's economy. The apostle Peter encourages wives to believe God will work in their husband's heart just by their example: "Wives, in the same way be submissive to your husbands so that, if any of them do not believe the word, they may be won over without words by the behavior of their wives, when they see the purity and reverence of your lives" (1 Peter 3:1-2).
God's Word does not tell a wife to keep hammering away at her

clueless and hard-hearted husband until he gets it. Nor does it encourage a wife to wallow in self-pity and despair until her husband breaks under the weight of witnessing her utter despair. Instead, it instructs wives to win their husbands without words—the end result of watching a life of purity and reverence lived out before them.

Author and apologist Lee Strobel was a hard-core atheist in the early days of his marriage. Working as a legal correspondent for the *Chicago Tribune,* he got a front-row seat to all the corruption, violence, and depravity a city the size of Chicago can produce. Such daily exposure to sin and pain only deepened his cynicism about people and God (if there was a God).

In the midst of his successful and expanding journalism career, an unexpected and unwelcome event occurred in his home. His wife became a Christian. His reaction to her newfound faith was anything but enthusiastic. He actually developed a sense of jealousy fearing that his wife's first love and loyalty now belonged to Jesus Christ rather than to him.

Instead of losing his wife's affection, something quite the opposite occurred in his home. His wife became more not less loving toward him; she became more respectful rather than condescending. Her gentle spirit served to smooth the hard and brittle edges of his life, and little by little, he was drawn to her Savior. Eventually the day arrived when Lee entered the church of his own will and soon thereafter met Jesus Christ. Today he has become a leading apologist for the Christian faith and has written a number of landmark books, such as *The Case for Christ* and *The Case for the Resurrection.*

How did such a remarkable turnaround occur? While it was ultimately the work of God's grace and lavish mercy, the Lord used the gentle and quiet heart of Lee's wife to win him over without words.

Our decision to obey God and keep a soft heart toward our spouse must not be based on immediate results or the progress we see in our mate. Things might actually get worse to start with. Rather, our decision to maintain a softened heart must be based on the witness of

Scripture. To do so, we will need to daily keep our eyes on the Right Person for encouragement: "Let us fix our eyes on Jesus, the author and perfecter of our faith, who for the joy set before him endured the cross, scorning its shame, and sat down at the right hand of the throne of God" (Hebrews 12:2).

6. A soft heart accumulates eternal rewards stored for us in heaven.

This final benefit is what best-selling author and marriage counselor, Emerson Eggerichs, calls the "Cha-Ching Principle."[3] The "Cha-Ching Principle" derives its name from the sound the old-fashioned cash registers made when they recorded a sale. It signified that a profitable transaction had been completed. What does this have to do with marriage and keeping a soft heart?

Each time we demonstrate unconditional love toward our wife or show unconditional respect toward our husband, an eternal reward is rung up and deposited for us in heaven.

Loving a difficult spouse for the sake of heavenly rewards is at odds with a culture that demands immediate satisfaction. The Internet revolution, with its high-speed connections and instant downloads, has only fed our appetite for immediate results and instant gratification. The idea that we should live for years with our difficult or distant spouse, yet treat them with unconditional love and respect, seems irrational if not ridiculous.

Yet the Scriptures repeatedly tell us our real reward is not in this life but in the world to come. Hebrews 10:35-36 assures us, "So do not throw away your confidence; it will be richly rewarded. You need to persevere so that when you have done the will of God, you will receive what he has promised." And Jesus makes this remarkable promise in the final pages of Revelation, "Behold, I am coming soon! My reward is with me, and I will give to everyone according to what he has done" (22:12).

What Our Light and Momentary Troubles Are Accomplishing

There may be today no visible reason or tangible encouragement for you to continue keeping your heart soft toward your spouse. You may have even reached the point where a change of heart seems all but impossible. Could we encourage you to maintain your soft heart for no other reason than that it will one day be richly rewarded when Christ returns to earth?

Difficult as this may be to grasp, magnificent and eternal rewards are accumulating in heaven for those who obey God's Word by unconditionally loving and respecting their spouse. Is that just wishful thinking? Listen to the Bible:

> Therefore we do not lose heart. Though outwardly we are wasting away, yet inwardly we are being renewed day by day. For our light and momentary troubles are achieving for us an eternal glory that far outweighs them all. So we fix our eyes not on what is seen, but on what is unseen. For what is seen is temporary, but what is unseen is eternal (2 Corinthians 4:16-18).

It may seem as though all your gestures of kindness, acts of compassion, and attempts at love have been wasted on your spouse. Their heart may seem as far away from yours as the east is from the west. Yet even this day as you have shown love or respect (Ephesians 5:25-33), something eternal has been occurring—your eternal reward has been steadily building.

The Compounding Interest of a Soft Heart

There is a true story of a pastor who never earned more than twenty thousand dollars a year his entire career. Yet he married and raised a family on his modest income and consistently put a small portion of his salary into a savings account. Near the end of his ministry he approached a financial consultant in his church with a simple question: "What would be the best thing to do now with my accumulated savings?" The consultant assumed he was talking about a modest sum.

He was shocked to learn the pastor had saved more than one million dollars.

The same compounding interest principle holds true of the reward we will receive in heaven if we keep our hearts softened toward our spouse. The returns may not be immediate or impressive to start with, but our faithfulness over a lifetime will produce a huge and lasting reward. We will one day hear these words from Christ Himself, "Well done, good and faithful servant! You have been faithful with a few things; I will put you in charge of many things. Come and share your master's happiness!" (Matthew 25:23).

While it may seem discouraging and even foolish to keep our heart softened toward our spouse when they fail to reciprocate, it's actually a winning game plan. It sets us up for a closer fellowship with God, it models the behavior that will give our children an edge in life, it will teach us valuable spiritual lessons, it will invite unexpected blessings from God into our life, and ultimately it will be the most powerful tool God can use to soften our spouse's heart.

It reminds us of a principle learned years ago, "You cannot do the right thing and ultimately have it turn out wrong. Nor can you do the wrong thing and ultimately have it turn out right. God's moral universe simply will not allow it to happen."

If we choose to keep our heart soft toward our spouse even when their heart is not, it can only turn out right in the end. The integrity of God's Word guarantees it:

> God is not a man, that he should lie,
>   nor a son of man, that he should change his mind.
> Does he speak and then not act?
>   Does he promise and not fulfill?
>
> (Numbers 23:19)

In the next chapter, we turn to the all-important question, "Is it sometimes too late to soften my heart toward my spouse?"

Lord Jesus, help me to live out a soft heart toward my spouse each day regardless of their response. Use my actions more than my words to model the life of Christ in our marriage. Let me resist every temptation to return wrong for wrong or evil for evil. Instead, help me to respond with love and acts of mercy rather than seeking payback or revenge. Establish healthy boundaries in our marriage that will safeguard love and respect between us. Help me to remember that a soft heart brings rewards both now and for eternity. Let me prepare for the day I will meet You face to face in heaven. When that day arrives, may I have no regrets for the way I lived my life before my spouse and children. Amen.

Questions for You and Your Spouse to Discuss

1. Why is it necessary for both spouses to soften their heart in order for The Marriage Miracle to occur? Does that mean it's useless for one spouse to take the first step and soften their heart?

2. Which of the six reasons for a spouse to keep a softened heart even if their partner does not seems most compelling to you? Why?

3. Why is watching a softened heart lived out each day in a marriage more influential than using words to persuade? What most impresses you about the way your spouse lives out their life day by day?

CHAPTER 8

Dealing with Heart Regrets

JANE WAS A PASTOR'S DAUGHTER who spent years as an adult partying, pursuing illicit relationships, and ignoring her own marriage and children. When she finally softened her heart toward God and her husband, she was overwhelmed with an emotion she didn't know what to do with—soul-searing regret.

"I wasted so much of my life," she confessed with tears. "I can never get those years back."

When It All Sinks In

What do we do with the regrets that inevitably result from years or even decades of a hardened heart toward God and our spouse? When it finally hits us—the enormity of the opportunities we lost, the squandered relationships, and the years we spend disconnected—how do we keep from being crushed by the weight of remorse?

Thankfully the Scriptures offer a way to deal positively with our regrets and losses. They show us a healing road where Christ will walk with us through the deep valleys of remorse and painful memories. On the other side is a place of consolation and even joy.

Is it too good to be true? Not when we look at the life of one biblical character who could have easily been crushed by the burden of his hard-hearted behavior. Instead, he found the forgiveness of God and even His blessing. His name is David.

A Dark Episode in an Otherwise Remarkable Life

David is described in the Bible as a person the Lord sought out to replace Saul as king of Israel. The Lord said he was "a man after his own heart" (1 Samuel 13:14). For the first half of David's life it was evident why God had chosen this young man to one day be king. He was a faithful shepherd, a valiant warrior, a caring husband, and eventually a righteous king. However, there came that fateful evening when he saw Bathsheba, the wife of one of his faithful army officers, bathing on a rooftop. Overtaken with lust he sent for the married woman and engaged in sexual intimacy with her. Bathsheba soon sent word back to David that she was pregnant with his child. That's when David devised a plan to cover up his sin and have her soldier husband, Uriah, ambushed and killed in battle. The plan worked, and Uriah was cut down defending Israel and for all appearances died a hero's death.

What David did not count on is what we so often fail to reckon with in our hard-heartedness—there is a God in heaven who sees everything we do.

Just as David and Bathsheba's love child was to be born, God sent the prophet Nathan to David with a message. Nathan told David a disturbing story about a rich man who stole the only lamb of a poor man. He used the lamb to feed his dinner guests, showing no remorse or twinge of conscience. David, incensed by such selfish and cruel behavior, jumped to his feet and shouted, "As surely as the LORD lives, the man who did this deserves to die! He must pay for that lamb four times over, because he did such a thing and had no pity" (2 Samuel 12:5-6). (It's curious how when we harden our hearts, we can see the faults of others so clearly and be so blind to our own sin and shame.)

That's when Nathan dropped the hammer, "You are the man!" (v. 7).

A Day of Reckoning Always Arrives

Sooner or later the things we've said and done in our hard-heartedness catch up with us. It may be when our wife announces she's leaving us because she can't take the belittlement or verbal abuse any longer. Or it may be when our children move away from us for good and rarely come home—they can't take our impossible perfectionism or lack of affirmation. Or perhaps it's when we come to the end of our days and realize we wasted our married life bickering and fighting.

When the full weight of our foolishness and sin comes down full force on us, it can be overwhelming. Regrets can strangle what's left of joy in life. With time no longer on our side, we can move to the very edge of despair. One wealthy businessman in our area spent his entire lifetime building his business career while neglecting his wife and marriage. When he learned that he was facing life-threatening lung problems, he chose not to have the surgery. "What's the use?" he said. "I have no close relationships. Why would I want to go on living any longer?"

It's Never Too Late to Revise

Thankfully, God has a plan to rescue us from our regrets. Even when we've squandered decades of our life and marriage on unworthy pursuits, in God's economy, as long as we're still alive, it's not too late. As Nancy Thayer once said, "It's never too late—in fiction or in life—to revise."

Let's go back to the story. David's heart, now broken and devastated by the realization of what he had done, confesses, "I have sinned against the LORD." Notice he engages in no excuses, no minimization of his behavior or blame-shifting to Bathsheba. It's a moment of genuine honesty and confession. He sees with clarity and understanding just what his hardened heart has done—he has seduced a married woman, murdered an innocent and loyal friend, and misused his authority as king. Perhaps his greatest insight is who suffered the most for his crimes,

> Against you [Lord], you only, have I sinned
>   and done what is evil in your sight,
> so that you are proved right when you speak
>   and justified when you judge.
>
> (Psalm 51:4)

David no doubt thought he was a candidate for swift and immediate justice. He had offended a holy God and had blood on his hands. Yet David's sincere change of heart (recorded for us in Psalm 51) touches the heart of God.

Here we find the overall truth of how we can deal with our regrets in marriage: *God will always respond to genuine humility, honesty, and confession regardless of how serious or heinous our heart crimes have been.*

The prophet Nathan, sensing David's willingness to admit and take responsibility for his crimes, conveys this word of grace from God to David, "The Lord has taken away your sin. You are not going to die." Though David would live to see the awful consequences for his behavior (including the death of two of his sons), he was given the assurance that God was going to spare his life. David experienced firsthand the truth of Proverbs 28:13,

> He who conceals his sins does not prosper,
>   but whoever confesses and renounces them finds mercy.

Seven Principles for Finding Freedom from Regret

We find seven principles from David's experience that we can apply to our own lives and find release from the burden of guilt and start our lives over again.

1. Acknowledge the bad decisions our hard heart made.

One of the most fruitful prayers we can ever pray is, "Lord, show me the wrong things I have done with my hard heart." Little by little, usually in doses we can take without choking, God reveals the sins of our brittle heart. His desire is for us to acknowledge our wrongs one at a time. As we agree with Him that what we did was contrary to His loving character and holy Word, we begin to experience the freedom and cleansing promised in 1 John 1:9, "If we confess our sins, he is faithful and just and will forgive us our sins and purify us from all unrighteousness."

2. Identify the spiritual problem that led to our wrongdoing.

Behind everything we've done to injure our spouse or children is a spiritual problem at work. Though we may have shouted or nagged our spouse, the primary sin is not verbal abuse but a heart driven by pride, control, or fear (or all three together). Once we get beyond our behavior and begin to examine the underlying sin and pain that a hard heart produces, we are on the road to freedom from bondage.

Jesus points to the heart as the source of all wrong behavior, "For from within, out of men's hearts, come evil thoughts, sexual immorality, theft, murder, adultery, greed, malice, deceit, lewdness, envy, slander, arrogance and folly. All these evils come from inside and make a man 'unclean'" (Mark 7:21-23). It's vital that we cut the root and not just the stem of our sin issues. Otherwise, they'll soon grow back, and we'll repeat the same destructive mistakes again and again.

3. Seek the forgiveness of God and of those we have hurt.

We've covered this basic principle in earlier chapters, but making amends where amends should be made is vital. It won't undo the wrong we've done to our spouse or the painful consequences it has caused our children, but we will be set free from soul-paralyzing guilt. When we ask the forgiveness of those we have hurt, it has a way of removing the barb from the hook of our past sins and memories. It allows us to move on with our lives and relationships rather than buckle under the enormous weight of regrets. That's why Proverbs 14:9 instructs us,

> Fools mock at making amends for sin,
>   but goodwill is found among the upright.

4. Resolve to make different decisions next time.

Not all regret is harmful or toxic to our souls. There is a type of regret that leads us to genuinely resolve to never make the same mistake(s) again. If that's what happens, then some good has come out of our bad experience.

Some time ago I (Bob) made a list called "Twelve Life Lessons Learned the Hard Way." Not each of the life lessons is original, but each has a special meaning and value to my life today:

- Nothing is ever gained by quitting (so never give up).

- Never burn your bridges behind you.

- Remember the wing-walking principle (don't let go of something you should hold on to until you grab hold of something else to hold on to).

- Stay in control of your emotions at all times and at all costs.

- A good name is much more to be desired than great riches.

- Remember there are more people counting on you than you realize.

- God is working right now in ways you don't know about.

- Listen to your friends before making any life-changing decisions.

- Never, ever feel sorry for yourself.

- Turn to prayer, praise, and thanksgiving to disarm every spiritual attack you face.

- In the midst of trouble, find a counselor or friend to help save your heart.

- Stay emotionally connected in the difficult times to your spouse and family.

As you might guess, there is a measure of regret over unfortunate choices that helped fashion each life lesson. Yet regret can be a wonderful counselor and teacher that burns indelible lessons into our heart. The pain and high price paid to learn those lessons can protect us against repeating similar wrong decisions in the future.

5. Remember that God's mercy triumphs over His judgment.

If all of us got what we had coming from the hard-hearted things we've done, precious few couples would make it to their fiftieth anniversary.

James 2:13 states, "Mercy triumphs over judgment!" Regardless of how guilty we are, how foolishly we may have acted, or how wicked our motivations have been, we still have the opportunity to experience God's forgiveness. David wrote a psalm that offers hope for every spouse who carries deep regrets:

> The LORD is compassionate and gracious,
>   slow to anger, abounding in love.
> He will not always accuse,
>   nor will he harbor his anger forever;
> he does not treat us as our sins deserve
>   or repay us according to our iniquities.
> For as high as the heavens are above the earth,
>   so great is his love for those who fear him;
> as far as the east is from the west,
>   so far has he removed our transgressions from us.
> As a father has compassion on his children,
>   so the LORD has compassion on those who fear him;
> for he knows how we are formed,
>   he remembers that we are dust.
>
> (Psalm 103:8-14)

For everyone who wrestles with deep regrets take real comfort: God will not pay you back as you deserve. If you are willing to repent (change your heart and mind) and turn to Him in faith, He will remove your guilt an infinite distance. Seeing our weakness and vulnerabilities, He views us with a Father's pity rather than a judge's contempt.

No Fear of Tomorrow

Many spouses who have treated their husband or wife poorly and at last come to realize it, struggle with a fear of the future. *What's going to happen to me once everything I've done catches up with me—particularly when I face God?*

Again, the Bible offers comforting news: "In this way, love is made complete among us so that we will have confidence on the day of judgment, because in this world we are like him. There is no fear in love. But perfect love drives out fear, because fear has to do with punishment" (1 John 4:17-18).

Though we may wish with everything in us that we had not lived with a hardened heart, once we receive life-changing salvation through Jesus Christ, we no longer need to fear a future day of judgment. Perfect love drives out all fear because Christ has already suffered for our sins—no future punishment is in store for us.

6. Learn from the pain and then let it go at the foot of the cross.

This principle is closely related to the previous one, but it gives us more specific instructions about what to do with our regrets. While our regrets can become great life coaches and masterful teachers, once we have fully learned our painful lessons it's time to graduate from UDR (the University of Deep Regrets). It's time to go on with our lives.

When a painful episode from our marriage comes to mind, how should we respond to it? It might be helpful to imagine a large Dumpster directly beneath the cross of Jesus Christ. Imagine taking the sin in your hard heart that led to a traumatic episode in your marriage and stuffing it in a large trash bag. Once it's all inside the bag, cinch up the tie strings, carry it over to the Dumpster, toss the bag inside, close the lid, and walk away.

Each time you experience another painful memory of what you said and did, go back to the cross and toss that memory into the same

Dumpster. When you open the lid and look inside, you'll find it's empty. All the trash you left there before is gone. That's because there's nothing left in God's economy of the hard-hearted sin that produced your regrettable behavior.

Paid to Perfection

How is it possible to know that when God empties the Dumpster, it's empty for good? Listen to the final words of Christ on the cross: "It is finished" (John 19:30).

Nothing more can be added or done to Christ's payment for our sins. The sins that we so regret in our marriage or family relationships have been paid in full. Once they are dropped into the Dumpster of Christ's forgiveness, they are gone for good. Search as you will, you will never find them again. Our debts have been erased and cleared for all time.

Colossians 2:13-14 describes this incredible process: "When you were dead in your sins...God made you alive with Christ. He forgave us all our sins, having canceled the written code, with its regulations, that was against us and that stood opposed to us; he took it away, nailing it to the cross."

Would You Chase a Garbage Truck?

It's important to leave our regrets behind and by faith go on with our lives. Can you imagine chasing a lumbering garbage truck down the street yelling, "Please come back! Don't take my trash away from me! I desperately need it for just a few more days!" We do just that when we refuse to let go of our painful regrets. Let God take them away for good.

The apostle Paul, personally responsible for violently persecuting Christians in his preconversion days, wrote later in his life, "But one thing I do: Forgetting what is behind and straining toward what is ahead, I press on toward the goal to win the prize for which God has called me heavenward in Christ Jesus" (Philippians 3:13-14).

There is a time and place to look long and hard at our regrets. We should learn from them all we can. Then there comes a time to cast them behind us and never look back. God has a high calling for us to fulfill, and we won't be able to fulfill that assignment unless we press on by forgetting what is behind.

7. *Trust God to take our worst decisions and turn them into an enduring blessing.*

Perhaps the most amazing aspect of how God deals with our regrets is what He finally does with them. Rather than permitting them to weigh us down like iron chains to drag through life, God transforms them into something else. That something else is a lasting blessing not only to us but to others as well.

Remember that though David was forgiven, the consequences of his sin exacted a heavy price. The young son born to David and Bathsheba died just seven days later. Yet God did not forget His promise to bless David. Eventually, God would grant to David and Bathsheba another son, this one named Solomon (which means "peace" in Hebrew). Solomon became God's choice to succeed his father as king of Israel. Even better, Solomon would ultimately build the magnificent temple in Jerusalem and make it the centerpiece of worship, praise, and prayer in all of Israel.

The Glory of God Descends

The day Solomon dedicated the temple the glory of God appeared,

> When all the Israelites saw the fire coming down and the glory of the Lord above the temple, they knelt on the pavement with their faces to the ground, and they worshiped and gave thanks to the Lord, saying,
> "He is good;
> his love endures forever."
> (2 Chronicles 7:3)

Though David and Bathsheba's relationship began in the darkest of sinful behavior, judgment did not have the final word—the grace of God did. God forgave their sin and used their offspring to build a temple filled with the Presence of God Himself.

My Way or God's Way?

Perhaps the most famous song of the legendary singer Frank Sinatra was titled, "My Way." Written by Paul Anka, it is considered by many to be Sinatra's musical autobiography. It is a blatant celebration of the fact he lived his life in an entirely self-directed manner. If all we can say at the end of our lives is that we did it our way, including how we handled our regrets, that's not much to boast about.

I'm more drawn to a lesser known songwriter, a woman by the name of Elvina Hall, who had a much different story to tell than did Paul Anka or Frank Sinatra. Let the words she wrote be the benediction to this chapter. Better yet, let it be the final word on the regrets you may still be carrying from years of living with a hard heart:

> I hear the Savior say,
> "Thy strength indeed is small;
> Child of weakness, watch and pray,
> Find in Me thine all in all."
>
> *Refrain:*
> Jesus paid it all,
> All to Him I owe;
> Sin had left a crimson stain,
> He washed it white as snow.
>
> For nothing good have I
> Whereby Thy grace to claim;
> I'll wash my garments white
> In the blood of Calv'ry's Lamb.

And now complete in Him,
My robe, His righteousness,
Close sheltered 'neath His side,
I am divinely blest.

Lord, now indeed I find
Thy pow'r and Thine alone,
Can change the leper's spots
And melt the heart of stone.

And when before the throne
I stand in Him complete,
I'll lay my trophies down,
All down at Jesus' feet.

It is finished.

Lord Jesus, I bring to You all the regrets I carry in life. I have said and done things, especially in my marriage, that I wish I could erase. I bring these painful regrets to the cross where You have promised to separate my sins as far as the east is from the west. Let me learn the valuable life lessons my regrets can teach me. Let me not repeat these same mistakes again. Take the worst moments of my past and transform them by Your grace into a blessing to others. Let me leave the past behind and live with hope for all the good things You are still going to do in our marriage. Amen.

Questions for You and Your Spouse to Discuss

1. Is it still a blessing to have a softened heart if the result is having to deal with heavy regrets for the way you acted? What happens to people who don't know what to do with the regrets in their life?

2. What can you learn from David's life concerning your own

ability to lead a good life, only to stumble badly? What else can you learn about God's gracious character?

3. Are there regrets that you need to take to the cross of Christ and leave in the Dumpster? What good has come from the more painful episodes of your life?

CHAPTER 9

Is It Too Late to Soften My Heart?

. . . . ⓒⓄ . . . .

ONE OF THE SADDEST DISCUSSIONS I REMEMBER was with a youth pastor (not from our church) who had decided to leave his wife and children. Though he claimed there was no one else in his life, I strongly suspected there was another woman he wasn't telling me about. Why the skepticism? I've come to believe Genesis 2:18 helps explain why men don't leave their wives to be alone: "The LORD God said, 'It is not good for man to be alone. I will make a helper suitable for him.'" Men by nature are not designed for solitary lives—they were created with an instinctive need for a life companion. So when they say they're abandoning their wife so they can be all by themselves, I don't buy it. What more often than not happens is a secret lover is waiting in the wings to replace wife #1 as soon as the coast is clear.

Headed for a Sun-Scorched Land

The youth pastor and I met in the foyer of a downtown concert hall and addressed the issue head-on. I pleaded, sometimes with tears, for him to consider carefully what he was doing. He would be giving up a ten-year marriage, three beautiful children, and his qualifications to lead God's people—particularly young people who looked up to him.

There was no biblical basis for the divorce, so he was placing himself in a position of rebellion against God's Word. Scripture warns that the rebellious will find themselves living in a dry and sun-scorched land (Psalm 68:6)—a place of true isolation and misery.

His response was to angrily point his finger in my face and say, "Look, I don't love my wife any longer. I'm tired of doing the right thing. I'm going to take care of my own needs for once. Besides, it's just your interpretation of the Bible that it's wrong to break my wedding vows. I don't find the wedding vows I took even listed in the Bible." There was nothing I could say or do to change his mind or heart. They were brittle as stone.

What a tragedy. Here was a gifted young man who once loved God and His Word, treasured his family, and was a true example to young people of a follower of Christ. The man I once knew with such a tender heart no longer seemed to exist. He divorced his wife, and eventually another woman (the one who didn't exist) appeared and they were married.

Shipwrecking Your Faith and Marriage

Is it possible to harden our heart toward our spouse so long and so deep that we reach a point where we have no desire to turn back? Can we calcify to the point where we ruin everything we have worked for? Some of you may worry that you or your spouse may have reached (or are getting close to reaching) the point where hardness of heart is at the terminal stage in your relationship.

Paul warned the young pastor Timothy, "my son, I give you this instruction in keeping with the prophecies once made about you, so that by following them you may fight the good fight, holding on to faith and a good conscience. Some have rejected these and so have shipwrecked their faith" (1 Timothy 1:18-19).

The Scriptures clearly say it's possible to deaden our conscience and shipwreck our faith (and our marriage as well). That's why it's so important that the moment we hear the voice of God warning us to turn back, we should respond immediately in faith and good conscience and not harden our hearts.

Where does this leave us if we are so disillusioned or bitter about our marriage that we feel nothing but contempt toward our spouse? What if our attitude is, if the marriage ends tomorrow, so be it?

Today Is the Day to Act

The central hope and message of this chapter is this: *As long as we have even the smallest desire to soften our heart, it's not too late to save our marriage.* If we will heed the conviction of the Holy Spirit and respond in humility and repentance, there is still time. That's why we should never put off doing tomorrow what God tells us to do today. None of us know whether we will have another day of life to make things right. James solemnly reminds us, "Now listen, you who say, 'Today or tomorrow we will go to this city or that city, spend a year there, carry on business and make money.' Why, you do not even know what will happen tomorrow. What is your life? You are a mist that appears for a little while and then vanishes" (James 4:13-14).

A Clear and Present Danger

What are the warning signs we may be headed toward a dangerously hardened heart? If we frequently have such thoughts as, "I honestly don't care what happens to my marriage anymore," or "Who cares what the Bible says, I'm ready to run my own life," or "I wish I would wake up tomorrow and find my spouse was gone" (one unhappy newlywed said just that). If these or similar negative thoughts are racing through your mind, then real trouble lies just ahead. These self-destructive ideas, if left unchecked, will lead to a truly hardened heart. Once we reach that point, heaven only knows what we are capable of doing next.

The Signs that It's Not Too Late

Let's consider how we can know God is still working with us and it's possible to change our hearts toward our spouse.

1. We are still willing to admit we have heart problems.

Even though distance, detachment, and apathy may have taken over in our marriage, if we're willing to acknowledge that we have problems that are at least partially due to our hardening heart, it's not too late to change.

Moments of conviction may come fewer and farther between, but they still impact us. When we see a sad expression on our wife's face or recognize the look of loneliness in our husband's eyes, it still stirs occasional sadness or remorse in our hearts. That's one indication it's still not too late to change.

The next time that happens we should immediately ask God to please give us another chance to develop a tender heart toward our spouse. We should plead with Him to not let us forget the conviction of the moment. We should implore Him by His mercy to let our heart love our spouse again. If we are willing to respond to God's prompting, we have the sure hope of this wonderful promise, "I will give you a new heart and put a new spirit in you; I will remove from you your heart of stone and give you a heart of flesh" (Ezekiel 36:26).

2. We can still see it's a sin to reject our mate.

While God understands how difficult marriage can be and has pity on us as a Father pities His children, we should never minimize the fact He takes sin seriously. *Scripture plainly tells us it's a sin to harden our heart and reject our spouse.*

In Matthew 19:6 Jesus warns, "Therefore what God has joined together, let man not separate." It is simply wrong to separate our hearts from our mate. It is wrong to develop bitterness, anger, and detachment and to allow these sinful emotions to divide what God has joined together for a lifetime.

Listen to this word of warning, found in the last book of the Old Testament, to guard our spirits so that we don't eventually break from our spouse.

> Another thing you do: You flood the LORD's altar with tears. You weep and wail because he no longer pays attention to

your offerings or accepts them with pleasure from your hands. You ask, "Why?" It is because the LORD is acting as the witness between you and the wife of your youth, because you have broken faith with her, though she is your partner, the wife of your marriage covenant.

Has not the LORD made them one? In flesh and spirit they are his. And why one? Because he was seeking godly offspring. So guard yourself in your spirit, and do not break faith with the wife of your youth.

"I hate divorce," says the LORD God of Israel, "and I hate a man's covering himself with violence as well as with his garment," says the LORD Almighty.

So guard yourself in your spirit, and do not break faith.

(Malachi 2:13-16)

It's hard to miss the seriousness with which God takes the marriage relationship. Just as Jesus warned against hardening our hearts, Malachi warns against breaking faith with our marriage partner. They are two different terms to describe the same phenomenon.

3. We still have hope (however slender) that God will bring true intimacy to our marriage.

If one spouse has lived for years and even decades with unhappiness and conflict in their marriage, they eventually come to an important crossroads. They must decide whether they will continue to embrace hope or give up altogether.

If they choose to give up, they are left with only one of three options: (1) get a divorce; (2) have an affair; or (3) live with an uneasy truce in the house. Some choose this third option for the sake of the children or to protect assets or out of religious convictions against the first two. Yet all three are discouraging choices, aren't they? It's like choosing between bad, worse, and worst, not necessarily in that order.

What about the other road—the one embracing hope that God

will work? It calls us to believe things will change and a better day is coming if we continue to patiently trust our heavenly Father: "Now faith is being sure of what we hope for and certain of what we do not see" (Hebrews 11:1). To live by hope is to live by faith—and living by faith is a sure sign our hearts can still be softened.

Faith believes God can do the impossible and looks forward to the day the impossible arrives. Is that ridiculous, wishful thinking? Or can God truly do what seems unachievable? While the following story is not about marriage, we hope the truths it conveys about the nature of faith and the miraculous God we serve will encourage you.

Lessons Learned from the Prodigal Puppy

When we adopted our collie named Bo (short for Boaz), he was just another ordinary three-month-old puppy. One day, a year or two after we adopted him, we let him out into our backyard to play. Later, when we opened the door and called him to come in, he didn't appear. We searched the yard and found no Bo. Despite calls to local veterinarians, animal shelters, and the police, no one had seen him. After several weeks of searching, we were forced into the sad conclusion our Bo was gone.

Nearly a year later the local police department called and said they had retrieved a collie that matched the description of our dog. But when we went to the animal shelter, we reluctantly concluded the collie they had found wasn't Bo. After that crushing disappointment, we decided to try and put Bo out of our mind. Sometime later I (Bob) came across his feeding dish while cleaning the garage and thought, "It's time to throw this away." But I chose to keep the dish—the last, slender strand of hope in a drama that seemed irredeemably over.

A full five years after Bo's disappearance our twenty-three-year-old daughter was home visiting us, and she told us she had had a most unusual dream: "Last night I dreamed I saw Bo playing in our backyard along with our other dogs." We all dismissed her dream as wishful thinking.

Three days later the phone rang. It was an animal control officer some eighty-five miles from our home. "We have found your dog."

"What?" I said. "That's impossible. Our dog has been gone for over five years."

"Well, sir," the officer replied, "our staff scanned the microchip embedded in his neck, and your name and telephone number came up. It appears he's been living in the wild for some time, but our veterinarian says he's in good health for a dog that's six years old."

That afternoon we drove the eighty-five miles to the animal shelter, none of us entirely willing to believe Bo was still alive. As we entered the facility, we were met by the officer and a reporter holding a camera. They ushered us back to the examination room where we would meet the dog. "Now be careful not to rush him," the officer said. "He may not remember you, and he could jump at you if you frighten him."

We all agreed to hold back and wait to see if indeed this was our dog.

None of us will ever forget what happened next. The room was packed with animal control officers, staff veterinarians, and office workers. After what seemed like forever, a shelter employee walked around the corner with a large collie on a short leash. The dog took one look at our son Brent and ran toward him. He jumped into his arms, and the two embraced.

The officer later told us that in twenty years, he had never seen a dog reunited with a family after being gone for five years.

Against all hope, Bo returned to us. When once all we had was an empty dish to hold on to, the impossible was now a reality—Bo had come home.

We tell this story because it's a powerful reminder that with God, nothing is impossible. He cares for every aspect of our lives. His eye is forever on the sparrow.

You may have little or no hope this day that your spouse will ever soften their heart toward you. We urge you to please not give up. As long as hope continues to live in your heart, it's not too late to see God work.

4. We still recognize the prompting of the Holy Spirit even in what may seem to be the last days of our marriage.

Once cynicism, anger, and doubt take over, it becomes increasingly difficult to recognize the urging of the Holy Spirit. As days turn to weeks and weeks turn to months and the months become years, we get to the point of believing the end of the relationship is inevitable. Nothing can prevent it now, and after wasting so many years on the relationship, why waste any further time?

Thankfully, God can change our hearts even in the eleventh hour. The story of the two thieves who were crucified next to Christ illustrates this principle:

> One of the criminals who hung there hurled insults at him: "Aren't you the Christ? Save yourself and us!"
>
> But the other criminal rebuked him. "Don't you fear God," he said, "since you are under the same sentence? We are punished justly, for we are getting what our deeds deserve. But this man has done nothing wrong."
>
> Then he said, "Jesus, remember me when you come into your kingdom."
>
> Jesus answered him, "I tell you the truth, today you will be with me in paradise."
>
> (Luke 23:39-43)

One criminal died with a hardened heart hanging right next to the one Person who could have saved him from eternal night. The other thief turned to Jesus in the final moments of his life and was ushered into paradise that same day. The condition of their hearts made all the difference in determining their destiny.

The Holy Spirit Is Praying for You

The same is true when it comes to marriage. God continues to use the Holy Spirit to examine what's going on in the deepest places of our lives and offer us one final chance: "And he who searches our hearts knows the mind of the Spirit, because the Spirit intercedes for the saints in accordance with God's will" (Romans 8:27). Proverbs puts it this way,

> The lamp of the LORD searches the spirit of a man;
> it searches out his inmost being.
>
> (20:27)

In His final effort to rescue our hearts and marriage, the Spirit of God may use a Christian counselor or pastor or wise friend to get our attention and show us things in our heart that we never recognized:

> The purposes of a man's heart are deep waters,
> but a man of understanding draws them out.
>
> (Proverbs 20:5)

What that person points out may not be all that pleasant, but it is life-giving:

> Wounds from a friend can be trusted,
> but an enemy multiplies kisses.
>
> (Proverbs 27:6)

WHY THE DEAFENING SILENCE ON DIVORCE?

Sin is not a popular concept in our culture. Perhaps because of the prevalence of divorce in our time many pulpits have fallen silent on Scripture's view of divorce and remarriage. It's more fashionable to focus on the inner pain and sense of loss divorce creates rather than pointing out that God's Word considers divorce for unbiblical reasons to be sinful and wrong.

There are often innocent parties in a divorce who desperately need and deserve the church's support and compassion. They have done nothing wrong, and for the church to treat them as if they have only adds insult to injury. We should always remember they are victims of someone else's ungodly choices, and if it were up to them, their marriage would have remained intact for a lifetime.

What about those who bear the responsibility of divorcing for unbiblical reasons? Can they find mercy and grace as well? A hymn reminds us, "There's a wideness in God's mercy..." That broad mercy can cover even the worst decisions and mistakes we've made if we humble ourselves, confess our sins, and seek Christ's forgiveness. It won't necessarily remove the sad consequences of our sinful behavior, but it will restore us to a right relationship with God. Sadly, the consequences of divorce can continue the rest of our lives and even into the next generation. That's why God's Word pleads with us to go a different route with our marital problems—softening our hearts toward one another.

Yet, while the church does need to preach that God will extend forgiveness and grace to those who divorce for unbiblical reasons, that message should not diminish the fact that God also hates divorce (not divorced people) for the damage it inflicts. That's why it is caring and compassionate for pastors to openly discuss the sin of unjustified divorce and share its painful and often lifelong consequences.

Divorce Creates More Problems than It Solves

In the many years I (Bob) have been doing marriage conferences, I have found less than a handful of people who have anything good to say about divorce. Instead, the overwhelming numbers of those divorced say it was the worst experience of their lives and to be avoided if at all possible. We need to communicate a similar message of sober warning to our young people or to those contemplating ending their marriage for nonbiblical reasons. Divorce inevitably creates more problems than it solves, and any solution that creates more problems than it solves needs to be set aside for something better.

I am frequently asked, "What are the biblical exceptions that allow for divorce and remarriage?" A legitimate difference of opinion exists among sincere believers as to what these exceptions are, or if they exist at all. From my study of Scripture and from the writings of those I highly respect, I believe there are just three:

1. Unrepentant adultery on the part of a spouse (Matthew 19:9)

2. Desertion by an unbelieving spouse (1 Corinthians 7:15-16)

3. If the divorce occurred before you were a believer (referred to as the "unmarried" in 1 Corinthians 7:25-28; cf. 2 Corinthians 5:17)

Every Word of God Is Flawless

There are cases where someone may be forced to divorce their spouse to protect their own safety and well-being and that of their children. These instances may include protection from a spouse's addictions, criminal activities, or seriously abusive behavior. While it is not a sin to divorce in such cases, Scripture says you are to remain single as long as your mate is alive, or if your ex-spouse undergoes a genuine change of heart, you should be reconciled to them (1 Corinthians 7:10-11,39-40).

Is holding to such high standards harsh, legalistic, and uncaring? That's the position taken in many quarters today. As a result, divorce and remarriage is allowed for virtually any and every reason. Yet if we are to be true to God's Word, we cannot invent exceptions where they don't exist; we are not given that prerogative. The Bible tells us,

> Every word of God is flawless;
>> he is a shield to those who take refuge in him.
> Do not add to his words,
>> or he will rebuke you and prove you a liar.

> (Proverbs 30:5-6)

As much compassion and understanding as we might have for a person trapped in a difficult marriage, it's never a caring or courageous thing for us to encourage someone to set aside God's Word to try to solve their problems. As difficult as it is for us to understand at times why God doesn't allow for more divorce and remarriage exceptions, we simply need to trust His wisdom and the loving authority of the Scriptures: "Heaven and earth will pass away, but my words will never pass away" (Matthew 24:35).

For those teetering on the edge of ending their marriage for unjustified reasons, Proverbs challenges us to care enough to plead with them to turn back before it's too late,

> Rescue those being led away to death;
>   hold back those staggering toward slaughter.
> If you say, "But we knew nothing about this,"
>   does not he who weighs the heart perceive it?
> Does not he who guards your life know it?
>   Will he not repay each person according to what
>   he has done?
>
> (Proverbs 24:11-12)

Let's Keep to Both the Horizontal and Vertical

When it comes to the subject of divorce and remarriage let's not make the mistake of focusing so much on the horizontal that we exclude the vertical relationship that exists between us and a holy God. The reason God hates divorce is that He is a holy God who loves people and a God who will not break His covenant. In His holy and loving character, He wants to protect people from heartache, deep pain, and a legacy of wounded families and children.

It's not just divorce that we need to say is wrong, but also the resentment, malice, and hardened heart that precedes it: "Get rid of all bitterness, rage and anger, brawling and slander, along with every form of malice. Be kind and compassionate to one another, forgiving each other, just as in Christ God forgave you" (Ephesians 4:31-32). A hard heart sets the stage for the breakup of a marriage, and it is an offense to God. That's why the Holy Spirit will spring into action and convict our hearts the moment these wrong attitudes enter our lives. It's a spiritual heart-check from our Friend and Advocate in heaven telling us to turn around before it's too late.

Only one remedy exists for sinful attitudes and words, and that's repentance. It requires us to respond to the prompting of the Holy Spirit and confess and turn from our wrongdoing. As soon as we do, new love, healing, and freedom start to flow into our hearts and marriage: "If we confess our sins, he is faithful and just and will forgive us our sins and purify us from all unrighteousness" (1 John 1:9).

On the other hand, if we push stubbornly onward in our sin, we take a step closer to the day when our hearts may be hardened beyond repair and our marriage lost.

THE ROLE OF CHURCH LEADERS IN SAVING MARRIAGES

Perhaps the most underutilized method God has given the church to soften hearts before it's too late is church discipline. Rampant individualism and a worship of personal privacy have made the idea of church leaders intervening in the life of someone caught up in sin seem altogether inappropriate, if not spiritually abusive. Yet what does Scripture say on the matter? "Brothers, if someone is caught in a sin, you who are spiritual should restore him gently. But watch yourself, or you also may be tempted" (Galatians 6:1).

Why should church leaders get involved in what seems to be a private matter? They can offer a listening ear, a caring heart, and the ministry of God's Word to help heal the relationship. If necessary, they can warn, correct, or even rebuke the erring person(s). Church leaders are charged by God Himself to protect the spiritual well-being of the congregation.

Paul's clear directives to Timothy, a young pastor in the church at Ephesus, underscore a leader's solemn responsibilities,

> In the presence of God and of Christ Jesus, who will judge the living and the dead, and in view of his appearing and his kingdom, I give you this charge: Preach the Word; be prepared in season and out of season; correct, rebuke and encourage—with great patience and careful instruction. For the time will come when men will not put up with sound doctrine. Instead, to suit their own desires, they will gather around them a great number of teachers to say what their itching ears want to hear (2 Timothy 4:1-3).

If a Marriage Suffers, Everyone in the Church Suffers

If caring, humble, loving, and godly leaders in churches today would take the risk of intervening in a Christian home headed toward self-destruction, there's no doubt many families could be rescued. While some might believe marriage and divorce are personal matters and none of the church's business, the Scriptures beg to differ. Listen to the teaching of Paul on the matter: "To the married I give this command (not I, but the Lord): A wife must not separate from her husband. But if she does, she must remain unmarried or else be reconciled to her husband. And a husband must not divorce his wife" (1 Corinthians 7:10-11).

Paul cites the prohibition against unjustified divorce as a command from the Lord Himself. Why such strong concern for marriages in the body of believers? The sin of one can impact the health of the whole: "If one part [of the church body] suffers, every part suffers with it; if one part is honored, every part rejoices with it. Now you are the body of Christ, and each one of you is a part of it" (1 Corinthians 12:26-27).

If an impending divorce between two believers is outside of Scriptural boundaries (recognizing there is often an innocent party), then it calls for church leaders to get involved,

Obey your leaders and submit to their authority. They keep watch over you as men who must give an account. Obey them so that their work will be a joy, not a burden, for that would be of no advantage to you.

Pray for us. We are sure that we have a clear conscience and desire to live honorably in every way (Hebrews 13:7-8).

"Where Was the Church When My Family Was Falling Apart?"

God will one day require church leaders to give an account for what went on in the church body under their watch. This includes the breakup of homes and marriages that could have been prevented if caring leaders had gotten involved. Not that a leader has any innate power or authority to prevent a divorce, particularly if one or both spouses' hearts have hardened. Yet it could be that the Holy Spirit will use the loving intervention of a deacon, elder, or other church leader to soften the heart of a couple preparing to break up their home (and the hearts of their children).

More than one adult child of divorce has later asked, "Where was the church when my parents' marriage was breaking up? They were both believers. Why didn't anyone get involved and try to stop this? Their divorce ruined my life, and the church leaders just looked the other way. Didn't anyone care what happened to me?"

If you are in a position of spiritual authority and leadership in your church, it's a question you ought to seriously ponder.

Reconcile to God, Then to Each Other

There is a biblical order in which God will soften our hearts. He will first soften our hearts toward Christ, then toward each other. The small epistle of 1 John underscores this truth: "But if we walk in the light, as he is in the light, we have fellowship with one another, and the blood of Jesus, his Son, purifies us from all sin" (1 John 1:7). The first step toward a changed heart is to walk in the light with God.

This light refers to letting God shine the light of His truth and grace on the sin hidden in our hearts. When we confess our wrongdoing to God and repent of it, we are then able to have fellowship and friendship with one another.

That means you have to soften your heart first toward God, then toward your spouse, regardless of how late it may be in your life or marriage.

Raised in the Final Days of the Wild West

Several years ago I discovered a small, out-of-print paperback titled *The Redemption of Paul Rader.* First published in 1915, it is the life story of one of the most influential men of God in early twentieth-century America.

Paul was the son of a Methodist circuit-riding preacher and was raised in the Wild West during the final days of the great frontier. When his father invited a group of soldiers from Fort Logan near Cheyenne, Wyoming, to visit their house, young Paul sat on the steps and listened to his father's sermon. At the conclusion of his father's message, "I went to my room, fell on my knees, and was sobbing," he later wrote.

His father found the young boy up in his room and tenderly said, "Now, my boy, let us tell Jesus what it is." That night Paul put his entire trust in Christ as his Savior and knew beyond a doubt that he had received the gift of eternal life.

A few weeks later a traveling bishop came to check on his father's missionary work and struck up a conversation with Paul.

"What do you intend to do with your life?" the bishop asked.

"I want to be a preacher," Paul said.

"Well, then, let us kneel here and ask God to make you a preacher."

Preaching to a Vacant Room

Paul waited until his sixteenth birthday to tell his father of his call to the ministry. His father decided to test the boy's calling by sending him on a train to a remote outpost on the prairie to preach to the cowboys. When Paul reached the town, he put up signs advertising services for the coming weekend to be held in the country schoolhouse.

The first Sunday morning Paul arrived to preach at the rented location, but no one showed up. Not to be deterred, Paul got up and announced the opening hymn to the vacant room. He then sat at the piano and played all three stanzas of the only hymn he knew.

He then stood up to preach to the thirty unoccupied chairs. Ten minutes into his first sermon, the back door burst open and in walked the landlady of the local boardinghouse, known far and wide as the toughest woman west of Cheyenne. She was accompanied by an elderly woman hard of hearing.

The young boy nodded in their direction and nervously continued with his sermon. Suddenly the landlady fell to her knees, "O my God, preacher, I repent," she cried out. She then began to pour out everything she had done in her sordid and difficult life. "Will the blood of Jesus save me?"

Young Paul calmly replied, "The blood of Jesus Christ cleanses from all sin."

The woman stood up and began to shout for joy. That afternoon she exhausted four horses riding through the county knocking on doors and asking forgiveness from everyone she had wronged.

A Desperate Telegram

By nightfall the streets were packed with cowboys, ranchers, and curious misfits who had heard something strange was going on in town. Paul had only one sermon and was going to preach it again when God prompted him to let the landlady tell her story. The woman delivered a testimony that would have melted a steel anvil in January. Conviction of sin and the power of the Holy Spirit fell on the room like a mighty wind. The town blacksmith jumped to his feet and shouted, "I want that kind of faith." He was followed by others all wanting God to come into their lives. Before the evening was out, nearly the entire town confessed their faith in Christ.

Paul wired his father, "I need help. Please come quickly." The older Rader was sure his son's life was in danger and took the first train to the remote outpost. When the train pulled into the station, all Reverend Rader could see was at least fifty of the locals gathered to meet him.

"Oh, no, it's a lynch mob." But as the doors to the train opened, he was welcomed with a chorus of "Just as I Am." Paul stepped out of the crowd and handed his father $175.

"Where did you get this money?" his father asked.

"It's from the offering last night," Paul said. "It's so we can build a church here."

That was just the beginning of Paul Rader's remarkable early years of ministry. He experienced one miracle after another as he traveled the West preaching the gospel.

The Modernists Ruin a Preacher's Heart

Paul Rader left the Wild West and entered seminary back East in the early 1900s. It was an era when many schools were starting to question the Bible's authenticity and authority.

The so-called "modernists" taught that moral education and not spiritual salvation was the answer to humanity's problems. They used their brilliant scholarship and impressive pedigrees to try to disprove the Bible's miracles, the virgin birth, and even the resurrection of Jesus Christ. Little by little, Paul found himself persuaded by their keen minds, fluent lectures, and impressive scholarship. His faith in Christ slipped away and with it the tender heart that God had used to spread the gospel.

Soon after his graduation from seminary, Paul took a church in Boston, but inwardly he knew he was a sham. He had lost his spiritual fire. He eventually quit the ministry and took a teaching post on the West Coast, then left teaching so he could travel in Europe.

A decade later Paul was married and the father of three daughters.

Yet his heart was not set on his wife and family but on making money— big money. He left his wife and family on the West Coast and traveled to New York City to arrange financing for a start-up oil venture that would make him a millionaire almost overnight.

But God was not through with Paul Rader's heart—not yet.

Tangled Up in Sin

One afternoon Paul was walking near Wall Street when he noticed a flashing neon sign above him. It depicted at first a cat playing with a ball of thread, then showed the cat all tangled up in the string.

"That's you, Paul," the Holy Spirit gently whispered. "You are all tangled up in sin."

Paul recognized that God was speaking to him, but he was not yet ready to soften his heart. Instead he completed the final business negotiations and wired his wife with the announcement, "Fixed for life." But a careless telegraph operator instead wired the words, "Fixed for like."

His wife immediately wired back, "Fixed for what?"

Her words hit Paul Rader with the force of a locomotive. That's right, what was he fixed for?

That's when he heard the voice of God more direct than ever, "Paul, if you will drop it all and follow Me, I will lead you into the truth and give you a message."

Three Days of Crying Out to God

Paul Rader went back to his hotel room and locked himself in for three days. He spent those hours crying out to God. On the third day, after he had confessed all the sin and rebellion of his hard heart, a softness toward God returned. "No human words can ever tell the joy that came into my heart when my sins, my failure, and my hypocrisy were dealt with by means of blood which I must call precious, the precious blood of Christ," he later wrote.

The next day Paul met with his business partners and broke off his share of the deal. He had only ten dollars left in his pocket. With a renewed sense of love for his wife and daughters, he sent all the money he had in the world back to them.

He soon returned to the work of preaching, and the power of God again descended on his listeners. Everywhere he went people were convicted of their sins and turned to Christ in faith. He became pastor of the Moody Memorial Church in Chicago and served there for several years. Eventually he could not resist the call of God to return to evangelism, the work of his youth. He packed out one meeting hall after another as he traveled across the United States.

God's Spirit working through the softened heart of Paul Rader and others led to the birth of numerous ministries that changed the spiritual landscape of the twentieth century: HCJB Radio, Slavic Gospel Association, Trans World Radio, New Tribes Mission, Youth for Christ, and AWANA Clubs International to name just a few.

The End Can Be Better than the Beginning

Paul Rader's story is a story for everyone with a hardened heart. Even though we may have lost our way with God, with our spouse, and with our children, even though we may have made some horrible choices and broken the hearts of those closest to us, God is not finished with us. He can soften our hard hearts even in the eleventh hour. He can give us a new love for Him and for our spouse. Our marriage can be rescued from years of neglect, stubbornness, and pride. The end can be even more remarkable than the beginning.

Is it too late to soften your heart? Not if there remains in you even the slightest desire or prompting to do so. If that's the case, thank God, it's not too late.

"Today if you hear his voice, do not harden your hearts..." (Hebrews 3:15).

> *Lord Jesus, please bring to my mind those things in my marriage that I need to make right. Don't let me harden my heart*

to the voice of Your Holy Spirit. Give me the courage to obey You and deal with the issues in my heart before it's too late. If I am headed in some wrong direction that could ultimately shipwreck my faith or my marriage, turn me around while there's still time. Use the Bible, other believers, and my own mate to help me hear the truth I need to hear. Thank You that Your grace and mercy will follow me all the days of my life. Amen.

Questions for You and Your Spouse to Discuss

1. Why is it a bad idea in marriage to keep putting off till tomorrow something you should do today? What are some things both of you have been putting off that need to be done now?

2. How can you tell when the Holy Spirit is prompting you to do something? Will God's prompting always be consistent with the teaching in God's Word?

3. What is God's order of reconciliation in relationships? Is there anything you need to reconcile with God in order to be reconciled with each other?

CHAPTER 10

Keeping a Soft Heart for a Lifetime

· · · · · · · · · · · · · · ◯◯ · · · · · · · · · · · · · · ·

SEVERAL YEARS AGO when our children were still quite young, I (Bob) took them to a Christian camp that has a petting zoo. We walked into the gated area and found goats, sheep, Shetland ponies, and, oh yes, llamas milling about us.

The children quickly noticed food pellets for sale in vending machines, and my pockets were soon emptied of quarters. The children were particularly interested in feeding the strange looking llama. The kids giggled with delight as they reached out their hand, and the llama nuzzled down the pellet. It looked like fun to me, but I was out of money to buy more pellets. I decided to do the next best thing—I would pretend that I had pellets to feed the llama. So I reached out my hand, and sure enough, the llama walked over, reached down, and nuzzled for food in my palm.

It took a moment for him to catch on to the scam, but once he realized he had been tricked, he took one or two steps back, reared up his head, and spit in my face. Suddenly my glasses went green (I've since learned that llama spit is actually bile).

I was momentarily stunned by this brazen display of disrespect. I did the only thing a self-respecting man would do in such a situation—I took one or two steps back, reared up my head, and spit back at the llama. It would be difficult to describe the look of astonishment on my children's faces. Later over lunch I heard them secretly whisper to Cheryl, "Mom, Dad spit at the llama this morning."

"Oh, your father has been under a great deal of stress lately," she said in my defense.

Pride—The Truly Original Sin

What causes a grown man to spit at a llama? I believe the answer is found in the same word that motivates couples to slam doors, exchange dirty looks, and threaten each other with lawyers.

That word is *pride.*

Pride is the ultimate cause of all human misery and suffering. Every ill on our planet—including a hard heart in marriage—can eventually be traced back to this, the original sin. The Bible is clear about pride's impact on our lives and close relationships,

> Pride goes before destruction,
> a haughty spirit before a fall.
>
> (Proverbs 16:18)

Have you ever stopped to consider what keeps us from being the first to apologize after an argument? Or what causes us to look at other men and women and admire their qualities while shaking our head in disgust at our own spouse? Or why couples choose to sit across the room and say nothing to each other for a day or week or even a lifetime?

That's right—it's pride.

If we are going to maintain a soft heart in marriage, we will have to daily battle and defeat the ultimate enemy of our relationship—pride. If pride hardens our hearts toward each other, then humility will soften our hearts as no other force on earth can. It can break down the highest walls and cross the deepest divides of our marriage relationship. It can change us from cold and distant partners to loving and intimate soul mates. It can even reconcile our children to us despite whatever alienation and hurt has taken place.

The Transforming Power of Going "One-Down"

What is humility? *It is unselfishly focusing on the needs of another person as an act of unconditional love.*

Humility will transform the atmosphere of our home from a refrigerated warehouse to a sunroom filled with radiance and laughter. Humility has the spiritual power to break through the hardest of hearts. Consider the apostle Peter's advice and how it could transform your marriage each day:

> All of you, clothe yourselves with humility
> toward one another, because,
>> "God opposes the proud
>>> but gives grace to the humble."
> Humble yourselves, therefore, under God's
> mighty hand, that he may lift you up in
> due time (1 Peter 5:5-6).

The positive impact of humility in marriage has even been studied by a major university. The researchers interviewed Ben and Hanna, a couple who participated in the study, and reported how humility operates in their marriage:

> Both considered humility to be about putting others first as expressed in the performing of small, thoughtful acts and not expecting anything in return. Both listed numerous examples, such as making supper, opening doors, and running bath water for the other...In addition, each identified "one-down" moves in situations where self-centered people might employ "one-up" moves. Examples included Ben's practice of not gloating (when he's right about something) and Hanna's decision to withhold judgment (when

Ben makes mistakes)...Each also referred to "protecting"
the other during times of unemployment and battling
cancer.[4]

Doesn't that phrase "one-down move" describe the heart and character of our Lord Jesus? His entire life—from birth in a lowly stable
to baptism in a muddy river to death on a cruel Roman cross—was a
"one-down move" so that we could experience a "one-up move."

If we are to maintain softened hearts toward each other, we will
have to live out this "one-down" attitude in the big and small choices
we make daily. Each time we show true humility toward our spouse,
we strengthen the bond between us. Even if you are living with a
spouse with a hardened heart, they will not be able to dismiss genuine
humility. As we've learned earlier, it may take much time and prayer,
but eventually true humility will break down your spouse's stubborn
and hardened heart.

Praise Is a Vote that God's Up to Something Good

Not only is humility vital to keeping a soft heart, but so is exercis-
ing daily a spirit of praise. One of the greatest discoveries is the power
praise unleashes in the midst of difficult circumstances.

We once went through an unexpected job loss. A downsizing move
left me (Bob) with only a few months to find a new job. It was tempting to give in to worry and despair, but Cheryl and I eventually made
the decision to praise God for this unexpected turn in the road.

Just a few weeks before my job was to end, I received a phone
call one morning out of the blue from a book publisher on the West
Coast. The editor asked if I was interested in coauthoring a book with
another author. I knew the author in question had just secured someone to help write the book, so I reluctantly had to pass. That's when
the editor came back with a most unexpected question: "Do you have
a book you'd like to write?"

"Well, as a matter of fact I do," I said. "It's a book about a marriage in the Old Testament that never should have been—between Jacob and Leah. Yet they turned out to be the ancestors of David, Solomon, Joseph, Mary, and ultimately Jesus."

"Send me a proposal," he said. "We'll look it over and get back to you."

They liked the idea, and a year later our first book, *For Better, For Worse, For Keeps,* was published. Little did we know that simple conversation would prove to be the beginning of a brand new chapter of our life and lead to our marriage ministry that continues to be the focus of our effort. By praising God in that difficult situation, one we didn't necessarily welcome or understand, He opened the door to a most fulfilling and satisfying new ministry.

Our tendency is to offer God praise only when we experience encouraging and happy circumstances: "Oh, thank You God for my new promotion," or "Praise the Lord, my medical test results were negative!" Yes, it's right and good to praise God for the good things that come our way. The Bible tells us, "Every good and perfect gift is from above, coming down from the Father of the heavenly lights, who does not change like shifting shadows" (James 1:17).

But what about praising God when our circumstances are discouraging or threatening? The psalmist David challenges us,

> I will extol [bless] the LORD at all times;
>   his praise will always be on my lips.
> My soul will boast in the LORD;
>   let the afflicted hear and rejoice.
> Glorify the LORD with me;
>   let us exalt his name together.
>
> (Psalm 34:1-3)

Did you catch the opening phrase? "I will extol the LORD at all times..." Not just when we are feeling particularly close as a couple. Not just when an unexpected refund check arrives in the mail. Not just when our children are living close to God. No, the Bible tells us we are to praise God at all times, even when we are living with suffering and affliction.

The New Testament makes this same call to praise God regardless of our circumstances: "Through Jesus, therefore, let us continually offer to God a sacrifice of praise—the fruit of lips that confess his name" (Hebrews 13:15). In practical terms this means we are to praise God when the two of us are on the same page or when we argue over every dollar spent. We are to praise God when we see eye to eye and when we just can't come to agreement. Why praise God for difficult moments in marriage? Isn't that a denial of reality, a foolishly naïve view of life, or even a waste of time?

No, praising God in dark and difficult moments is a key to keeping our hearts softened toward each other. When we praise the Lord, something changes in the condition of our hearts, even if nothing changes for now in the condition of our marriage. Praise is our vote that God is up to something good in our relationship regardless of our present circumstances.

Have You Tried Praise Lately?

Years ago, when I was going through a difficult season of life, someone gave me a copy of the devotional classic, *Streams in the Desert*. This enduring work was written by Mrs. Charles Cowman, the wife of a missionary in the Far East at the turn of the twentieth century. It was written from her own painful experiences as a means to encourage hurting and discouraged believers.

One story that affected me was about a missionary in China who was ready to throw in the towel. Before leaving China to return home, he decided to take an extended sabbatical at a mission station. He arrived at the guesthouse with a plan to spend weeks in prayer, introspection, and wrestling with God regarding his future in China. Instead, when he opened the door to his room, he happened to glance up at the wall and saw a simple plaque that read, "Have you tried giving thanks?"

The question hit him with the force of a Pacific typhoon. Right there he dropped to his knees and began to give God thanks for all the difficulties he faced. One by one, he let go of his anger and self-pity and began to embrace thanksgiving and praise.

The hosts were admittedly surprised when the next day their visiting guest stood at their door with bags packed. A radiant smile on his face, he announced he no longer needed a month of sabbatical to sort through his problems. God had lifted his depression, and he was ready to dive back into his work.

I can't guarantee that you as a couple will experience such an immediate turnaround in your marriage the moment you begin giving God thanks and praise for your difficult circumstances. However, a heart that turns from anger and self-pity to forgiveness and thanksgiving will soon find the sun breaking. Psalm 34 shares the ultimate result of praise:

> I sought the LORD, and he answered me;
> > he delivered me from all my fears.
> Those who look to him are radiant;
> > their faces are never covered with shame.
> This poor man called, and the LORD heard him;
> > he saved him out of all his troubles.
>
> (34:4-6)

Turn to praise and thanksgiving as a husband and wife when things are difficult. It will keep your hearts soft toward each other and toward God. It will open the opportunity for God to demonstrate His grace and free you from the cruel prison of gloom and hopelessness.

Caring for Each Other's Heart

Another method to maintain a soft heart toward God and our spouse is to care daily for our spouse's heart. There is great power in caring for another person:

> Hatred stirs up dissension,
> but love covers over all wrongs.
>
> (Proverbs 10:12)

The apostle Peter continues the theme of this proverb when he says, "Above all, love each other deeply, because love covers over a multitude of sins" (1 Peter 4:8).

The term *covering* refers to providing a remedy or solution to erase a debt of sin or wrongdoing. It's similar to going out to eat with someone, and when the bill comes, they reach over and say, "The bill is mine. I've got it covered." Love covers all wrongs and sins the same way a fresh coat of paint covers a faded wall or a scented candle covers the odor in the kitchen.

Regardless of whether our mate's heart has been abandoned, rejected, defiled, detached, immoral, or worse, love can cover their pain. It will restore, renew, and heal what's been badly damaged in their heart. The apostle Paul makes this claim, "And now these three remain: faith, hope and love. But the greatest of these is love" (1 Corinthians 13:13).

Ten Minutes a Day Will Change Your Marriage

The implication of this truth is profound for keeping a soft heart in marriage. That's why choosing to care for our spouse's heart is one of the most vital things we can do to create and maintain an emotionally intimate and fulfilling marriage.

How can we care daily for each other's heart? *The way to care for your spouse's heart is to speak directly to their heart.* (I've included in Appendix 6 some questions from John Regier's outstanding workbooks to help facilitate this process for you.)

We do not believe in the existence of some "inner child" often espoused by secular counselors. Such notions are false and unbiblical. But we do believe that if a child experiences something traumatic or painful at a certain age, their heart may lock up at that point. Even though they grow up in other areas of their life, their emotional heart may remain stuck at that stage of life. It helps explain why a grown spouse can at times act like a little child. They are acting out of an emotional heart that is still immature. If they are behaving five years old, it may be because at age five their heart was traumatized.

The gospel is good news for people with damaged hearts. When we allow the healing power of Jesus Christ to repair our damaged hearts, and when we find forgiveness toward those who have hurt us, our arrested hearts can develop to their proper age. It may take weeks or even a few months, but the healing power of love can transform a twelve-year-old heart to the forty-five-year-old heart it should be. As the Bible promises, "Love covers over a multitude of sins." Love allows a heart to grow and develop as God designed it to be.

While it first and foremost is the love of God in Jesus Christ that restores damaged hearts, He will also use the love of our spouse to assist in this healing process. That's why caring for your spouse's heart is so vital. You can be God's instrument in the healing and restoration of their heart by protecting, loving, and seeking out their innermost thoughts, feelings, and desires. No one on earth is more equipped to care for your spouse's heart than you are.

Speaking the Language of the Heart

God has put you in each other's life for a reason. While pastors, counselors, and caring friends can do a great deal to help heal your husband or wife's heart, no person can do more for your spouse's heart than you. It happens when we speak words of love, compassion, acceptance, and care to our spouse's heart.

The Song of Solomon is a poem of deep and intimate married love. It paints a word picture of how two married lovers can speak to each other's heart as no one else can:

> You have stolen my heart, my sister, my bride;
>   you have stolen my heart
>   with one glance of your eyes,

with one jewel of your necklace.
How delightful is your love, my sister, my bride!
How much more pleasing is your love than wine,
and the fragrance of your perfume than any spice!

(Song of Solomon 4:9-10)

Like an apple tree among the trees of the forest
is my lover among the young men.
I delight to sit in his shade,
and his fruit is sweet to my taste.
He has taken me to the banquet hall,
and his banner over me is love.
Strengthen me with raisins
refresh me with apples,
for I am faint with love.

(2:3-5)

Whenever we speak directly to our spouse's heart in a caring and intimate way, our marriage is changed. How can we speak directly to our spouse's heart? Again, I've included some material from John Regier in Appendix 6 that encourages couples to set aside some time to care for each other's heart—to sit down and face each other, look into each other's eyes, and ask probing questions such as:

- Have you ever felt loved? If so by whom?

- Have you ever given your heart to me?

- Have you ever felt rejected? By whom?

- Do I take time to listen to the needs of your heart?

Speaking directly to our spouse's heart can even stop an argument dead in its tracks. In the midst of the tension, take your spouse's hands in yours, look into their eyes, and say in a calm and loving voice, "I'm so sorry I was cross with you. I ask your forgiveness because protecting your heart means so much to me. I think the world of your heart and would never want to do anything to damage it. Your heart is precious to me. Is that okay with you?"

It's hard to imagine the argument going on much longer. Remember, God created us to have childlike hearts, not childish hearts (Matthew 19:13-14). When we treat our spouse's heart with the same love, tenderness, and concern we would treat a child's heart, we will see a positive response.

Ask Simple Questions

I have seen couples who once thought their marriage was all but over melt into each other's arms and a sea of tears as they began to speak caring words to each other's heart. The Bible assures us it's God's desire to restore damaged hearts,

> The LORD is close to the brokenhearted
> and saves those who are crushed in spirit.
>
> (Psalm 34:18)

When we choose to care for each other's heart, we align ourselves with God's purposes. The result is His blessing and presence in our relationship in a unique and powerful way. As you do so, watch how previously destructive patterns start to disappear as each heart feels genuinely loved and secure. Even depression, anxieties, and a host of other emotional issues will begin to draw down as we care for each other's heart. When we choose to speak directly to our husband's or wife's heart, we can watch love do its amazing work. The Bible tells us,

> Keep your heart with all diligence,
> For out of it spring the issues of life.
>
> (Proverbs 4:23 NKJV)

The issues of our life are found in the heart. As we care for each other's heart, we will be able to maintain a soft heart. We will begin to experience a depth of love and intimacy only God could give us.

The Encouragement of Accountability

To maintain a soft heart toward one another requires accountability in our lives. Even after we've softened our hearts, there is always the danger of drifting back into old routines and habits unless someone encourages us and asks hard questions. The Bible says, "But encourage one another daily, as long as it is called Today, so that none of you may be hardened by sin's deceitfulness" (Hebrews 3:13). One key to maintaining a softened heart is to encourage each other daily.

Not only do we need to affirm all the wonderful character traits we see in each other (such as the childlike attributes of forgiveness, trust, kindness, caring, and acceptance), but we should invite our spouse to tell us if they see us returning to old habits. We should give them permission to tell us if they see us once again believing the deceptions and lies that once hardened our hearts. If they see our hearts headed in the wrong direction, they should have permission to tell us the truth. The Bible counsels,

> He who listens to a life-giving rebuke
> will be at home among the wise.
>
> (Proverbs 15:31)

> Let a righteous man strike me—it is a kindness;
> let him rebuke me—it is oil on my head.
> My head will not refuse it.
>
> (Psalm 141:5)

The New Testament calls us to mutual accountability: "Therefore confess your sins to each other and pray for each other so that you may be healed. The prayer of a righteous man is powerful and effective" (James 5:16). If we come to trust and love each other deeply, we won't be easily offended or angered when our spouse points out a trend that could be leading to a hardened heart. We'll welcome such concern and respond by dealing with our heart issue in prayer and repentance.

One couple that was used to engaging in heated arguments discovered the value of stopping the confrontation and instead trying to understand what was going on in the heart of their spouse. The tension dropped dramatically in their marriage. "We've learned there is a different road for us to walk down when we disagree. Now we don't end up in the same place we always did. Just knowing one of us is sensitive to the pressure of expectations and the other is sensitive to abandonment issues has helped us care for each other and calm one another down when we're upset." This couple learned the secret of accountability, helping each other avoid falling into the same old traps that had nearly destroyed their marriage.

The Secret to Daily Heart Success

Perhaps the most important thing we can do to keep a soft heart is to maintain daily intimacy with God. We should practice regular times of prayer and Bible study that allow the Holy Spirit to convict us of sin and unbelief the moment it enters our heart. That way we can quickly confess our sin to God and ask Him to restore a childlike heart to our life and marriage.

Vonette Bright, the widow of Bill Bright, founder of Campus Crusade for Christ, was once asked what the secret was to her husband's remarkable life. She responded, "His emphasis and teaching on the Holy Spirit."

The Holy Spirit is the ultimate secret to maintaining a soft heart in marriage. The Holy Spirit will restore the love, joy, peace, patience, kindness, goodness, faithfulness, gentleness, and self-control we need to keep our hearts soft and let our marriage prosper (Galatians 5:22-23). Once the Spirit of God is in control of our hearts, we can disagree with our spouse but do it in an agreeable way. Let's examine how the Holy Spirit can help us have an agreeable disagreement.

Nine Ways to Have a Fair Fight

The Bible in fact gives us the ground rules for disagreeing or "fighting" with soft hearts:

> Therefore each of you must put off falsehood and speak truthfully to his neighbor, for we are all members of one body. "In your anger do not sin": Do not let the sun go down while you are still angry, and do not give the devil a foothold...
>
> Do not let any unwholesome talk come out of your mouths, but only what is helpful for building others up according to their needs, that it may benefit those who listen. And do not grieve the Holy Spirit of God, with whom you were sealed for the day of redemption. Get rid of all bitterness, rage and anger, brawling and slander, along with every form of malice. Be kind and compassionate to one another, forgiving each other, just as in Christ God forgave you (Ephesians 4:25-32).

Based on this biblical advice we can find several helpful ground rules for disagreeing in an agreeable fashion when conflict enters our marriage.

1. Speak the truth in love.

Regardless of what needs to be said, we can always say it with kindness. There is never a need to be harsh, cruel, or humiliating. Nor do we need to hide or conceal the truth from each other simply to keep the peace. When we speak the truth in love, relationships are preserved and important values are protected.

2. In your anger, do not sin.

Though our partner may have hurt or offended us, a softened heart will never seek to punish or shame or control the other person. If our expectations have been disappointed, we can still resolve the issue in a way that honors God and preserves the relationship.

3. Don't let the sun go down on your anger.

A softened heart will always seek to resolve the relationship rupture as soon as it occurs. While it is sometimes advisable to take a time-out when emotions are running high, we should never put off the reconciliation of our relationship to the next day.

4. Don't give the devil a foothold.

Unkind and unloving words or actions can give ground in our marriage to the enemy of our souls. At first he seeks only a toehold, then a foothold, then an arm hold, and ultimately a stranglehold. As soon as we realize we have damaged the other person's heart, we should seek forgiveness and reconciliation. Remember the nine words that Cliff Barrows said can rescue any marriage: "I am sorry. I was wrong. Please forgive me."

5. Don't use any unwholesome words.

If you must argue, then discipline your words. Don't say anything you (or your partner) will later regret. That means deciding ahead of time that you will never use certain words in an argument, such as, "I hate you," or "I regret the day I married you," or "I want a divorce."

6. Say only those things that will build up your spouse.

It is possible even in a conflict to use only positive and edifying words. In the midst of your disagreement you can interject statements such as, "That's an excellent point," "You have great wisdom," and "I have only the highest respect for you." Such positive and edifying statements will drain the toxicity from your disagreement and replace it with love and respect.

7. Don't grieve the Holy Spirit with your words or attitude.

It's important to remember that when you are arguing, Someone else is listening—the Holy Spirit who lives in both of you. Just as children's hearts are grieved when they hear their parents' argue because of a love and commitment to both, the Spirit of God is sorrowed when He hears us tear each other down. Say only those things to each other that would be pleasing to God. He is listening.

8. Forgive each other as Christ has forgiven you.

As difficult as it can be to offer forgiveness to our spouse, we need to remember that Christ has forgiven us not some or most but all of our

sins. If it were not so, we would have no hope of ever entering heaven
(not even a single sin will be permitted there). To forgive as Christ has
forgiven us means to forgive each other for everything.

9. Ask God to continually examine your hearts.

Even in the midst of a conflict with our spouse we can silently
pray,

> Search me, O God, and know my heart;
>   test me and know my anxious thoughts.
> See if there is any offensive way in me,
>   and lead me in the way everlasting.

> (Psalm 139:23-24)

The real issue is not whether we ever argue with each other, but
if we will allow God to keep our hearts soft toward each other as we
disagree. As God points out our wrong attitudes or hurtful words, we
can confess and repent on the spot.

In our marriage conferences I'll have a little fun with participants
by illustrating what a Spirit-filled, fair fight might look like:

"Dear, I need to say something to you that's been eating away at
me. I think you are really a generous and kind person."

"Oh really? Well, people tell me behind your back that you are
patient and compassionate. So what do you think of that?"

"While we're bringing up what others think, you should know
your mother told me you're longsuffering and merciful. She told me
you've always been that way and there's nothing she could ever do
about it."

"So now we're bringing up each other's family members are we? Well,
your family has a reputation for being hospitable and accepting."

I hope you can see the abiding truth behind the imaginary silliness.
If we said things to one another only to build each other up, using
only wholesome words with the intent to benefit the other person,
our arguments would take on a very different flavor—one that God
would be pleased with.

We Have a Friend in Heaven Praying

To summarize what we've learned, a softened heart is not a once-for-all achievement. Softened hearts in marriage need to be nurtured and maintained daily. Thank God we have an Advocate in heaven, Jesus Christ the righteous (1 John 2:1), who is always praying for us:

> For we do not have a high priest who is unable to sympa-thize with our weaknesses, but we have one who has been tempted in every way, just as we are—yet was without sin. Let us then approach the throne of grace with confidence, so that we may receive mercy and find grace to help us [and soften our hearts] in our time of need (Hebrews 4:15-16).

A woman was asked by a reporter if her late husband was perfect. She thought for a moment and said, "No, he wasn't always perfect. But whenever he was imperfect, he didn't stay that way for very long." That's a great explanation of how intimacy with God can help main-tain intimacy with our spouse. When we do get out of line, God will correct our heart and that allows us to go back to our spouse and make things right. Even when we are imperfect our hearts don't have to stay that way for long.

Thankfully we have a great friend in the Holy Spirit, who will con-vict us of hard-hearted attitudes and restore a desire to stay in tune with Christ and each other.[5] Furthermore, when our desire is to keep a soft heart toward our spouse we have all of heaven on our side. Imag-ine the bleachers of heaven filled with a cloud of witnesses who are "doing the wave" on behalf of your marriage. God's authority, power, and will are on the side of the two of you keeping a soft heart. With such powerful support from on high maintaining a soft heart can be a wonderful and continuing reality in your marriage.

In the final chapter we'll examine nine powerful and biblical rea-sons why keeping a soft heart toward one another matters so much to God. They will likely include reasons you've never considered before, but they impact you, your family, and the world around you.

Lord Jesus, the Bible tells me You oppose the proud but give grace to the humble. I don't want You to have to oppose any aspect of my life. Let me live with genuine humility before You and my spouse each day. Reveal to me each and every place that pride has slipped into my heart or marriage. Replace it with a Christ-like willingness to live "one-down" rather than "one-up" with my mate. Let me care for my spouse's heart each day by speaking words of comfort and care. Bind our hearts together with love and intimacy. I invite You, Lord Jesus, to replace self on the throne of my heart this day. Amen.

Questions for You and Your Spouse to Discuss

1. What are the various ways pride can work its way into your relationship? Why is humility such a powerful and attractive trait?

2. Why is it necessary to work at keeping a soft heart? Are you ready to speak directly to each other's heart on a daily basis?

3. Why do you need the Holy Spirit to keep your hearts right with each other?

CHAPTER 11

Why Two Softened Hearts Matters to God

I (Bob) was fortunate to be raised in the same church in Minneapolis, Minnesota, for almost two decades. Our senior pastor, Dr. C. Philip Hinerman, served a remarkable multiethnic congregation for thirty-seven years. When he retired, I went back home to the dinner held in his honor. The evening was a joyous tribute to his remarkable ministry and almost seven hundred people turned out for the celebration.

At one point people were given the opportunity to share what they most appreciated about Dr. Hinerman's nearly four decades of ministry. Those who went to the microphone recognized his powerful preaching, farsighted commitment to serving the inner city, and the numerous young people he mentored into the ministry (I was one of those fortunate individuals).

Yet the outstanding accomplishment heard most often was this: "I'd like to thank you, Pastor, for the way you loved your wife. Your marriage was an example to all of us." Person after person expressed their gratitude for the love and tenderness he displayed toward his wife,

Adora. One person said, "You may not have known this, Pastor, but your marriage offered hope when our own relationship was in trouble. Your example gave us the courage to keep trying."

Isn't that remarkable? After thirty-seven years of strong preaching, compassionate outreach, and visionary leadership, people appreciated most the quality of his marriage. That makes sense when you consider the high priority God's Word gives to a loving and intimate marriage.

WHY A LOVING MARRIAGE IS IMPORTANT TO GOD

The Bible gives at least nine reasons why a loving and intimate marriage, characterized by softened hearts, is so very important to God. Taken together, the Scriptures point us toward one overarching and compelling conviction: *Loving our spouse should be our first priority after loving Jesus Christ.*

The impact of our marriage on the well-being of the church, our family, and those around us makes the stakes incredibly high. If we allow God to soften our hearts toward each other, the reverberations will spread far and wide—to our children, to our neighbors, and even to the world. But if we harden our hearts, we can do irreparable damage to a wide variety of people.

Let's look at those nine biblical and compelling reasons why loving our spouse should be second in importance only to our love for the Lord Jesus.

Reason 1

A loving marriage is the first of all human relationships created by God.

The Scriptures tell us that the very first bond God designed on earth was between a husband and a wife: "So the LORD God caused the man to fall into a deep sleep; and while he was sleeping, he took one of the man's ribs and closed up the place with flesh. Then the LORD

God made a woman from the rib he had taken out of the man, and he brought her to the man" (Genesis 2:21-22).

This is a profound statement that the foundational relationship in all of life and society is marriage. While other relationships are important, none can compare to the primacy and importance of one husband and one wife connecting their hearts for a lifetime.

The Foundation of Any Society

It is from this mysterious and life-giving bond that all other meaningful relationships follow. What society or culture long survives when the basic building block of marriage is removed? We need look no further than the Shakers, a religious order of the eighteenth and nineteenth centuries in America, with origins in England. As a matter of doctrine they taught strict celibacy and forbade marriage. By the early twentieth century, this otherwise noble group of people had dwindled to two elderly adherents. Sadly, without marriage and procreation, all that was left was their legacy of finely crafted furniture and deserted buildings, which later became popular tourist attractions.

Whether in society as a whole or in a particular subculture, when marriage is no longer the first priority in relationships, that culture will eventually decline and finally fade from the picture altogether.

To follow God's priorities, we need to give first and foremost attention to our marriage relationship. *Therefore, loving others before we love our spouse distorts God's priorities.* When our first love is our work, our relatives, or even our children, we have skewed God's order and plan for our lives. Things won't work right in the church, our homes, and ultimately the world around us if our marriages are neglected or fail altogether. Can anyone seriously deny that many (if not most) of our society's current ills stem directly from the breakdown of marriage in the last fifty years?

It's Okay to Love Your Spouse More than the Kids

Children instinctively crave the security of knowing their parents love each other first and foremost. Yes, they may blush whenever we show open affection toward our spouse, yet inwardly they enjoy every moment of it. It ties a rope of assurance around their hearts that is not easily broken. That's why the best gift you can give your child is not an expensive video system, a new car, or a luxury vacation. The best gift you can give (after sharing your faith in Christ) is to love your spouse. It will anchor your children's hearts and lives for a lifetime.

Our oldest son, Robby, surprised me last year by writing an e-mail that simply said, "I want to thank you and Mom for loving each other and staying together. Thank you for giving us that example." Children find comfort in knowing their parents love each other (however imperfectly) and are committed for the long haul. It gives them a sense of belonging, an established identity, and a sure foundation as they take their place in the world. Research study after study confirms this truth.[6]

No relationship in the world offers a more nurturing and stabilizing impact on children than a loving, intact, two-parent family. Studies prove children from these homes excel beyond their peers in almost every area: school, jobs, self-discipline, and the list goes on. However, where homes are conflicted or the marriage breaks up, it has just the opposite impact on children. They struggle with low self-esteem, poor grades, lack of discipline, lack of respect for authority, and so on.

There's a reason for this. God created marriage as the first and foremost of all human relationships. That's why it's vital that we honor and cherish our marriage daily. We need to give the person we're married to our first and best each and every day, second only to our devotion to Jesus Christ.

Never Too Late to Revise

If that's not been the case in your marriage, it's not too late to change. As long as you both are still married and can recognize the prompting of the Holy Spirit, you can change course. You can make your marriage your first priority and begin to positively influence your children, grandchildren, and great-grandchildren whatever their age. Where to start? We'll make some practical suggestions at the end of the chapter to intentionally make your marriage your first priority in life.

Reason 2
A loving marriage uniquely reveals the glory of Christ.

As we learned in a previous chapter, the very first time Jesus revealed to the world that He was God come in the flesh was at a marriage celebration: "On the third day a wedding took place at Cana in Galilee...This [changing water to wine], the first of his miraculous signs, Jesus performed at Cana in Galilee. He thus revealed his glory, and his disciples put their faith in him" (John 2:1,11).

Of all the places or settings Jesus could have inaugurated His public ministry, He chose a wedding reception. Why not in the temple in front of the high priest or in the royal court in front of King Herod? Why not in the crowded market of Jerusalem or on the Stone Pavement entrance to Pilate's hall of justice? Why of all places a wedding reception in a remote village in northern Galilee? What is the meaning and message in choosing this location?

Jesus' presence at this wedding is neither a random nor an incidental appearance. It fits into the much larger scheme as a center point between the beginning of human history (the wedding in the Garden of Eden) and the end of history (the Wedding Supper of the Lamb) found in Revelation.

At this simple peasant wedding celebration, the great mystery of Christ's divine identity and His mission to sacrifice for His bride, the church, is first revealed. Marriage is Scripture's chosen analogy to explain Christ's deep and abiding love for His church. The apostle Paul explains the mystery further:

> Husbands, love your wives, just as Christ loved the church and gave himself up for her...In this same way, husbands ought to love their wives as their own bodies...After all, no one ever hated his own body, but he feeds and cares for it, just as Christ does the church..."For this reason a man will leave

his father and mother and be united to his wife, and the two will become one flesh." This is a profound mystery—but I am talking about Christ and the church (Ephesians 5:25-32).

Here for the first time at a wedding in Cana, Jesus' disciples are allowed to see His divine glory. John Piper and others have observed that marriage's ultimate purpose is to exemplify and glorify the work of Christ in the world. The Methodist Classical Wedding ceremony recognizes the amazing significance of Christ's attendance: "Marriage is a holy and honorable estate which Christ adorned and beautified by His presence at a wedding in Cana of Galilee."

Even the details of a story like this one have much to teach us when they fit into the larger body of truth and doctrine that Scripture teaches. Christ attends a wedding because the glory of the Messiah is uniquely reflected to us through the beauty and holiness of marriage.

In the same way, when our marriage is characterized by sacrificial love and care for one another, Christ's glory is reflected through our home to a watching world. We end up preaching the gospel of Jesus Christ with and without words through our marriage. As people behold His glory and grace lived out in our lives, it creates in them a desire to have the same thing occur in their marriage. It causes what could be called a holy envy—a longing to experience the very same peace, harmony, and unity. The glory of Christ thus shines through a loving marriage to a needy world.

On the other hand, an unloving marriage robs Christ of the opportunity to display His glory. Few things discredit the gospel as much as two professing believers who have an angry, unloving, and distant marriage. It quickly negates their witness of faith and instills doubt and cynicism instead.

One young man admitted he got drawn into a sexually immoral relationship at work out of discouragement after years of watching his parents' loveless and angry marriage. Though they professed to be Christians, behind closed doors they were openly hostile, bitter, and unforgiving toward each other. He eventually gave up hope that being a Christian could affect a marriage. That's when he decided to pursue a relationship with a nonbeliever.

Something similar happens each time a prominent pastor or Christian leader is caught in sexual immorality. A skeptical and cynical world shakes its head in disgust, "I knew all along there's nothing different about Christians. Forget what they preach, look at the way they live. They're just like everyone else."

Yet the world can be positively influenced when the glory of Christ is revealed in two believers with softened and accepting hearts. Billy Graham was married to Ruth Bell Graham for six decades. On the day of her memorial service, he looked down into his wife's casket and said, "Look at her today. She is still the most beautiful woman in the world to me." In that tender and sacred moment, the glory of Jesus Christ was revealed to the world.

That same glory can be shined through the prism of your marriage if you give your relationship the same priority God intended when He created the first marriage in the Garden of Eden.

Reason 3

A loving marriage teaches us about the future blessings of heaven.

There is something about a caring and committed marriage God uniquely uses to help us understand the coming glory and happiness of heaven. "Then the angel said to me, 'Write: "Blessed are those who are invited to the wedding supper of the Lamb!" ' And he added, 'These are the true words of God'" (Revelation 19:9).

Over and over again throughout Scripture, God uses the language of love, romance, and marriage to describe the exquisite joys of the world to come. In the book of Revelation we find expressions such as, "your first love," "the wedding supper of the Lamb," and "as a bride beautifully dressed." All these images are intended to teach us lessons about the life to come, one filled with the same exhilaration, joy, and celebration we experience at a wedding.

We experienced a little taste of the future blessings of heaven in our own family. When our oldest daughter, Melissa, was married, there was a spirit of joy and worship that transcended the moment. Many others there told us they too experienced a "rise above the moment" during portions of the service. How did that happen? As we worshiped the living Christ, He entered into the event and displayed His glory. With all credit to Christ Himself, the wedding turned into a taste of what awaits us at the future and glorious wedding supper of the Lamb.

Looking Forward to Death Do Us Part?

If a loving and joyous marriage can teach us about the life to come, unfortunately a failing and contentious marriage can sour us against the idea of heaven. It can make the wedding supper of the Lamb something to dread rather than anticipate. After all, who wants to be trapped in the celebration of a loveless and empty relationship for all eternity?

There are no doubt spouses reading this who actually look forward to the day when "death do us part." They have lived so many years in an unhappy and unfulfilling marriage, they look forward to being released from their wedding vows. The notion that heaven would be an unending replay of their marriage on earth makes them cringe. Isn't that a tragedy?

That's why it's so important that we make our marriage a first priority, one we enjoy with loving, tender, and joyful hearts. It will point people to the future and magnificent reality of heaven, where we will enjoy being with Christ and each other forever.

Reason 4

A loving marriage makes an effective prayer life possible.

The Bible makes the profound statement that how we relate to our spouse has a direct impact on our ability to communicate with God: "Husbands, in the same way be considerate as you live with your wives, and treat them with respect as the weaker partner and as heirs with you of the gracious gift of life, so that nothing will hinder your prayers" (1 Peter 3:7).

You almost have to read that verse a second time to absorb its full impact. God's Word says that if a husband fails to show his wife proper consideration and respect by treating her as coheir of the gift of eternal life, then God will not hear or answer his prayers. It's as if our heavenly Father has a cell phone, and when we mistreat our wife, He simply turns it off for now. We can keep calling, but He's not picking up.

Trying to Do Christianity Without Prayer

How many of us can successfully live the Christian life of witnessing, serving, giving, teaching, and loving if God doesn't answer our prayers? Can we possibly accomplish anything of eternal value without the power of God flowing into our lives? The answer is obvious. Without answered prayer, we are stopped dead in our tracks until we reconnect with God.

This leads us to a sober and alarming conclusion: *A harsh and argumentative marriage relationship empties prayer of its power.*

More than once during my years as a pastor, a Gentle Voice would interrupt my thoughts just as I was about to leave my church office to begin the worship service: "Bob, before you go out and preach, don't you think you need to call your wife and apologize for the way you spoke to her at the breakfast table?"

I would squirm in my chair but eventually pick up the phone. "Cheryl, I need to ask your forgiveness. How I acted this morning wasn't right. I really can't go preach until you forgive me and this is resolved." I'm thankful she always would extend her forgiveness.

I then felt energized. I could sense God's presence and help, something absolutely vital to preaching. The term for this is *liberty*. It means God is free to work and speak through our hearts because nothing is hindering His activity in our lives. The place to establish and maintain that type of freedom starts at home and with our marriage.

If we don't make showing consideration, respect, and honor to our spouses a first priority, the Bible warns that we can pray, but no one's answering. That's just too high a price to pay.

Reason 5

A loving marriage qualifies you to manage God's household.

Building on what we have just learned, God's Word is clear that things have to be in order at home for things to be in order in the church: "[An elder or church leader] must manage his own family well and see that his children obey him with proper respect. (If anyone does not know how to manage his own family, how can he take care of God's church?)" (1 Timothy 3:4-5).

For some reason we talk ourselves into believing that God wants us to give our first and best efforts to the church and that He's pleased with us serving leftovers of our time and energy at home. We can even find biblical texts that seem to support this idea. After all, didn't Jesus say, "I tell you the truth, no one who has left home or wife or brothers or parents or children for the sake of the kingdom of God will fail to receive many times as much in this age and, in the age to come, eternal life" (Luke 18:29-30). If that isn't a clear call to abandon our marriages and families for the sake of the church, what is?

A Much Different Conclusion

It's an important and accepted principle of studying Scripture that we let the Bible interpret the Bible. This requires gathering all the relevant teachings in Scripture on a topic and applying those teachings to the biblical passage in question. This becomes especially important when we are studying a difficult passage such as Luke 18.

Is Jesus calling us to daily abandon or forsake our families to pursue ministry? If we allow Scripture to interpret Scripture in this case, we come to a much different conclusion. Though it was Peter who said to Jesus, "We have left all we had to follow you!" (Luke 18:28), in his apostolic ministry he did not abandon his marriage. How can we know that? The apostle Paul, a contemporary of Peter and fellow apostle, gives us an eyewitness account of how Peter and the other leaders lived: "Don't we have the right to take a believing wife along with us, as do the other apostles and the Lord's brothers and Cephas?" (1 Corinthians 9:5). Paul reports that Cephas (Peter) and the other apostles regularly took their wives along with them in their ministry.

And as we noted earlier, this same Peter advised the believers under his pastoral care, "Husbands, in the same way be considerate as you live with your wives, and treat them with respect as the weaker partner and as heirs with you of the gracious gift of life, so that nothing will hinder your prayers" (1 Peter 3:7).

Balancing Radical Discipleship and Loving Stewardship

Did Peter say one thing but live another? Not when you understand the historical and theological context of his statement, "We have left all we had to follow you!" Peter did have to leave everything to follow Jesus as a disciple. He had to abandon his business, the traditions of the Jews, and his acceptance by religious leaders in order to follow Christ. That was the cost of *radical discipleship.*

Jesus calls us to be ready to make the same sacrifices today. If push comes to shove and the choice is between forsaking Christ or our family, we must remain faithful to Jesus. However, absent that type of extreme pressure or circumstance, we are to daily live out a *loving stewardship* of the spouse and family God has placed in our lives.

Christians who fail to understand we are called to both radical discipleship and loving stewardship will eventually find their marriages in serious trouble. It's one thing to endure prison to remain true to Christ; it is altogether a different matter to skip our anniversary dinner to attend another board meeting. Remember, Scripture calls us to manage our own households well before we attempt to manage God's household.

Leadership Integrity Begins at Home

More than one Christian leader has waked up to discover their marriage is in shambles and their ministry is falling apart because they neglected their home life. Things didn't arrive at that sad place overnight. It took years of sending their spouse and children to the back of the line. It's only then they discover this sad truth: *A neglected or chaotic marriage undermines your integrity as a leader.* (Interestingly, this same principle is now being recognized in the secular world. Business seminars for executives are teaching that a strong marriage at home is a prerequisite for being a strong leader at work.)

God's Word is clear that if we want to serve the church with love and integrity, we must first serve our family with love and integrity. There are no shortcuts or escape clauses that allow us to neglect our relationships at home and still be an effective Christian leader. When we fail to recognize this truth, the results can be tragic.

I (Bob) stopped at a gas station one day, and while I was paying for the purchase, the man on duty asked me what I did for a living. I told him I was a pastor. He said he was a first-generation immigrant with an Eastern religion upbringing. He said he almost had become a Christian and was even ready to be baptized by a local pastor—until that pastor ran off with his secretary. He waved his hand dismissively. "That day I lost all interest in becoming a Christian."

I wonder if the pastor who ran off with his new love interest understands the true cost of his actions. Perhaps if this pastor's priorities had been right at home, the gas station attendant would be sitting in his church today. What an enormous price we (and others) pay when we fail to make our marriages our first priority.

Reason 6

A loving marriage fulfills God's desire for godly offspring.

Of all the reasons to make our marriage our first priority, this one comes near the top of the list: "Has not the LORD made them one? In flesh and spirit they are his. And why one? Because he was seeking godly offspring. So guard yourself in your spirit, and do not break faith with the wife of your youth" (Malachi 2:15).

Notice that the passage begins by saying it is God who makes us one with our spouse when we marry. Oneness is a virtue that God highly values. The first and most important commandment in the Old Testament is, "Hear, O Israel: The LORD our God, the LORD is one" (Deuteronomy 6:4). While oneness has a variety of implications, it certainly speaks to the essential unity and harmony of the Father, Son, and Holy Spirit. The members of the Trinity never argue with one another, stage power plays, or act out passive-aggressive behavior. They live in a continual state of love, harmony, and trust.

What's the Big Deal About Oneness?

God wants this same oneness to be present in our marriages, but for what reason? Scripture tells us at least one of the reasons is so we will produce "godly offspring." That is, the unity in our marriage will influence our children to grow up to love and worship God just as we do.

Did you ever stop to consider the first Bible our children ever read is their father and mother? They gain their first and often enduring impressions of the character of God from watching us. If our marriage is loving, kind, and harmonious, they will find it much easier to believe in a loving, kind, and harmonious God.

Unfortunately, the opposite is also true. If our marriage is conflicted, angry, and mean-spirited, our children will come to see God that way. They will associate the character of God with the hostile and selfish behavior they see in our relationship. This leads to a serious reality we cannot ignore: *A troubled marriage produces troubled kids.*

A simple review of research studies done on the impact of divorce on children confirms this tragic and disturbing reality. While it is possible for children from troubled homes to grow up and build healthy marriages, they face additional emotional and spiritual obstacles in getting there. Many of these barriers could have been avoided altogether if their parents' marriage had been characterized by the oneness God desires.

Staging a Market Rally

We can think of our marriage as the Dow Jones Industrial average and our children as the S&P 500 or the NASDAQ index. As the Dow goes up, so typically do the other markets. As the Dow plummets, the lesser markets follow suit in short order. If your marriage is doing well, generally speaking your kids will end up doing well (there are exceptions). However, if you harden your hearts toward each other and division is the order of the day, it won't be long until your children are acting out similar negative behavior and attitudes.

Jim and Isabella went through a particularly bitter and difficult experience in their lives. Jim's heart turned hard against God, his wife, and other believers. It didn't take long for Jim's children to begin losing interest in church, running around with the wrong kind of friends, and even getting into mild trouble with the law.

Thankfully, Jim woke up to the fact that his bitterness was destroying his home. He decided to change course before it was too late. Jim went first to God and then to Isabella to seek forgiveness. Then he went to each child and asked his or her forgiveness for his sinful attitudes and bad example. That's when a miracle began to occur.

One by one, each of Jim's children began to come back to God, to their family, and ultimately to the church. Today, Jim's children love Christ. His family had reached the precipice of destruction due to his hardness of heart. He discovered the hard way that a troubled marriage produces troubled kids. But because he was willing to soften his heart and return to oneness with his God and his wife, his home was saved.

Much Bigger than Just the Two of You

Making your marriage your first priority has implications that go way beyond the two of you. The welfare and destiny of your children also hangs in the balance. That's why Jesus warns us to be ever so careful in the example we set for children: "But if anyone causes one of these little ones who believe in me to sin, it would be better for him to have a large millstone hung around his neck and to be drowned in the depths of the sea" (Matthew 18:6).

Thankfully, if we live with softened hearts (or return to that place) and exemplify in our marriage the love, harmony, and unity of the Trinity, we will give our children the best opportunity they will ever have to follow in our footsteps of faith.

> Train a child in the way he should go,
> and when he is old he will not turn from it.
>
> (Proverbs 22:6)

Reason 7

A loving marriage fulfills God's design for permanent relationships.

God's Word is abundantly clear that He desires a married couple to spend their entire lifetime together: "Haven't you read," [Jesus] replied, "that at the beginning the Creator 'made them male and female,' and said, 'For this reason a man will leave his father and mother and be united to his wife, and the two will become one flesh'? So they are no longer two, but one. Therefore what God has joined together, let man not separate" (Matthew 19:4-6).

One reason God is so interested in the permanency of our marriage is that everything about His character is permanent. God's love for us is permanent. Heaven is our permanent home. The Word of God is a permanent pillar that endures for all time. Because we are made in God's image, He desires that our marriage reflect His same permanence.

Do Your Relatives Despise Your Spouse?

The implications of this truth are many. God doesn't want our work or career to separate us. He doesn't want our in-laws or family members to separate us. He doesn't want competing schedules or different financial goals to separate us. Most of all, He doesn't want our hard hearts to separate us. Unfortunately, far too many couples allow others to separate what God has joined together.

One afternoon I was on a radio call-in show where the topic was, "Do your relatives despise your spouse?" The producer and I weren't sure if anyone was going to respond. Maybe we had chosen too narrow a topic. It didn't take long, though, for us to find out how wrong we were. Less than ten minutes into the program the switchboard lit up with one distraught listener after another sharing heartbreaking tales of in-laws, siblings, and parents driving a wedge between them and their spouse. One man tearfully admitted that pressure from his family led him to divorce his wife.

Sadly, so many couples fail to stand their ground on God's basic rule for marriage: "For this reason a man will leave his father and mother and be united to his wife, and they will become one flesh" (Genesis 2:24). They pay a huge price for ignoring the vital truth that paying more attention to others than your spouse will ultimately separate what God has joined together. That's why it's so important we make our marriage our top priority. Only then can we achieve and preserve the permanency that God desires.

Reason 8

A loving marriage is an avenue for God to bring salvation to the world.

Have you ever stopped to consider how the Christmas story could have happened without the loving and committed marriage between Joseph and Mary? While God could have sent His only Son into the world in any manner He desired, He chose to do so through a tender-hearted and steadfast marriage.

Not only does a strong marriage uniquely reveal the glory of Christ, but it can also be used by God to bring the Good News of salvation to others. This general principle still holds true today, though not in the exact same sense that it did for Mary and Joseph. God still uses loving and committed couples to bring the message of salvation to the world.

This was certainly true in Courtney's case. Raised in a single-parent home following her parents' divorce, she carried in her heart a deep sadness and pain that followed her into her young adult years. A young married couple invited her to live in their home while she attended college, and during the year and a half she stayed there, this couple lived out the love of Christ toward each other and toward her. As they did, God began to work in her life.

Eventually, Courtney decided to follow Christ and serve Him with her life. Later, she met a wonderful Christian young man, and the two were married and today serve Christ together. While it is God who brought healing and salvation to Courtney's life, He used a loving and committed marriage as His instrument to reach her with the message of salvation.

I Like Your Christ, I Do Not Like Your Christians

Unfortunately, once again the opposite is also true. *A failing or loveless marriage can become a stumbling block to effective evangelism.* When people sense only acrimony and bitterness in the marriage of two Christians, it creates confusion. They hear that this couple professes love for God, but what they see is that they don't really love each other. This disconnect creates enormous resistance to the Good News of Jesus Christ. One of the famous statements attributed to Mahatma Gandhi is, "I like your Christ; I do not like your Christians. Your Christians are so unlike your Christ."[7]

Let's not make it difficult for people to believe the gospel of Jesus Christ. Rather, let's make our marriages a high priority and live out our days with softened hearts toward each other. As we live and act like our Christ, people will desire to meet our Christ.

Reason 9

A loving marriage is a powerful witness to God's amazing grace.

A loving and forgiving marriage can become a living example of the daily operation of grace, "The LORD said to me, 'Go, show your love to your wife again, though she is loved by another and is an adulteress.

Love her as the LORD loves the Israelites, though they turn to other gods and love the sacred raisin cakes'" (Hosea 3:1).

One of the primary reasons marriages fail is that people believe it's impossible to come back from the deep hurt they experienced when there has been a betrayal in the marriage. They feel it's impossible to start over again. They can't conceive how the past injury can be erased or the two of them could possibly start over again. They conclude there's simply too much water over the dam and divorce is the only option left.

A Different Ending to Your Story

While I understand how deeply wounded spouses can feel that way, the testimony of Scripture offers a very different option than divorce or separation. The prophet Hosea was the victim of multiple betrayals by his openly adulterous wife, Gomer. He had every right according to Old Testament law to divorce her and have her sent away (Deuteronomy 24:1-4).

Yet, in the midst of Hosea's anguish and heartbreak, God shows up and urges him to use this moment to teach the nation of Israel an important truth. He is a God who is willing to forgive and to offer His people unmerited grace. He instructs Hosea to go and show love to his wife once again. Though she has known many lovers, he is to take her home, restore her place of dignity, and love her as his wife. He is to extend forgiveness and mercy rather than demand punishment and banishment. Hosea thus becomes a timeless example of God's amazing grace.

Following a marriage conference, the host pastor introduced me (Bob) to a middle-aged couple from his church. He told me their marriage was a true miracle and asked them to tell me their story. I listened as the husband explained that several years ago he fell in love with a much younger employee at work. He was flattered by her interest in him and got involved with her. Eventually he divorced his wife and left her to care for their two children all on her own.

Despite the unspeakable anguish and hardships his ex-wife experience, she continued to pray that God would one day restore their marriage. Just two years into his new marriage, the young wife walked into their living room and announced she was leaving him for someone else. She promptly filed for divorce.

At that moment the husband realized just what a fool he had been. He had abandoned the wife of his youth for a mid-life office fantasy. He had severed the trust of his children and humiliated himself by his selfish behavior. Humbled and broken, he came home with hat in hand and pleaded with his wife to give him another chance. Despite all that she had endured, she chose to do what God chooses to do—she offered him grace and a chance to start over. The two were reconciled, and their marriage stands today as a living example of the amazing grace of God.

Grace—Don't Leave Home Without It

We don't have to commit adultery to be in need of grace from our spouse. The everyday hurts and slights and wrongs we do to each other all require grace and forgiveness to be resolved and healed. A marriage cannot survive a lifetime unless both parties learn the secret of giving and receiving grace. How else can we go on when we have failed or hurt each other?

When people ask us how we made it to our thirtieth anniversary, we both respond with one word—grace. As the author of the hymn, "Amazing Grace," wrote long ago,

> Through many dangers, toils and snares,
> I have already come;
> 'Tis grace hath brought me safe thus far,
> And grace will lead me home.

Whenever you extend grace and forgiveness to your spouse, you are testifying to others who have made mistakes that there is hope for them.

Unfortunately the opposite is also true. *An unforgiving marriage sends the message to others there is no hope if you've made serious errors.* It reinforces the idea that once you have failed your spouse, you can expect only judgment and rejection. Fail them enough times and there's no way out of your mess and no road to travel back home.

No Pit Is So Deep

God's Word says there is no sin so heinous or so unimaginable that God's grace cannot remove it from our record of guilt. As the apostle Paul says, "But as people sinned more and more, God's wonderful grace became more abundant. So just as sin ruled over all people and brought them to death, now God's wonderful grace rules instead, giving us right standing with God and resulting in eternal life through Jesus Christ our Lord" (Romans 5:20-21 NLT). As Corrie ten Boom, a heroic underground worker and Holocaust survivor, once said, "No pit is so deep that His love is not deeper still."

If you are willing to maintain a soft heart toward each other, your marriage can serve as a living and powerful example of the grace of God.

Some Practical Suggestions to Put Your Spouse First

In closing, here are some simple suggestions to help make loving your spouse a top priority, second only to your relationship with Christ. Remember, giving your marriage the time and attention it deserves truly matters to God. He will help you implement these steps if you are willing to order your life and marriage according to His will.

1. Pray together before the day begins.

As we learned earlier, couples that pray regularly together experience less than a 1 percent divorce rate. Daily bring your marriage, children, financial needs, spiritual obstacles, and other concerns to God together in prayer. The Bible assures us heaven is always open: "Let us then approach the throne of grace with confidence, so that we may receive mercy and find grace to help us in our time of need" (Hebrews 4:16). Making prayer a priority in your marriage will invite

God's love and presence into that day's events. It will glue your hearts together as you worship the God who created your marriage.

2. Act out love to experience feelings of love.

One of the mysteries of keeping a softened heart is that we must continue to act that way even when we don't feel that way. When our emotions are upset or difficult to control, we need to still speak and act with a softened heart. Even if we are out of sorts, our feelings will eventually catch up with our right actions. Love is an action word in Scripture, not an emotion: "For God so loved the world *that he gave* his one and only Son, that whoever believes in him shall not perish but have eternal life" (John 3:16). God's love was demonstrated by His actions, not His emotions. The same is true for us. If we will act and speak lovingly, our hearts will overcome our feelings, and love will carry the day.

3. Spend thirty minutes a day in a shared activity and intimate conversation.

It's a truism that men communicate as the result of a shared activity, while women view communication as the activity itself. For example, if you want your husband to talk to you, then you should both engage in some simple activity such as walking, biking, or working on a project together. You'll find that sharing an activity with your husband will open him up to interact with you in a way he doesn't when sitting at the kitchen table. Make spending thirty minutes together a top priority so that you can stay connected through intimate conversation.

4. Give your spouse the right to access you any time day or night.

One of the important ways to communicate the priority your spouse is in your life is to allow them to interrupt your schedule. When I (Bob) was a pastor, I gave my secretary instructions to put my wife's telephone calls through any time day or night (and that of my children as well). Regardless of who I was meeting with, I was willing to take at least thirty seconds to talk to my wife. It was my way of communicating to Cheryl and everyone else that my marriage and kids were the first priority of my life. Of course, there were moments when I had to ask

Cheryl if I could call her back later, but the important point had been established that she comes first.

5. *Submit your time decisions to the fifty-year rule.*

It's a good idea to stop and evaluate the way the two of you allocate your time each day. The fifty-year rule simply asks, "Fifty years from now will we be glad or regret the way we used our time today?" Will the two of you make wise choices regarding your use of time? Or will you let the tyranny of the urgent drive your schedule? How we spend our time is perhaps the surest indicator of what we value most in life.

A father who kept a diary once wrote, "Wasted the whole day fishing with my son. Didn't catch a thing." Later in life he discovered the diary his son kept from that same period of their lives. Opening it to the same date, he read, "Went fishing with my dad. Best day of my entire life."[8]

Let's make sure we stop and evaluate how we spend our time with those closest to us—starting with our spouse. We won't have this life to live a second time. Once gone, the hours and minutes given to us cannot be regained. We will either use them to build cherished memories or to leave a blank space in our souls. We will use them to connect our hearts for a lifetime or to leave us lonely and separated. We will either value them for all eternity or squander them for all time.

We need to take this advice of Scripture to heart,

> Teach us to number our days aright,
>   that we may gain a heart of wisdom.
>
> (Psalm 90:12)

Our marriages all come with an expiration date. We may have only this day to connect our hearts; tomorrow may not come. We need to ask God to give us the wisdom to see our marriage as He sees our marriage. Once we do, we will make it the first and highest priority in our lives after our relationship with Christ.

"Today, if you hear his voice, do not harden your hearts…"

Lord Jesus, thank You for making it so clear in Your Word that my marriage relationship is to be among my highest priorities, second only to my devotion to You. I ask You to forgive me for allowing other things to confuse that divinely ordered plan. Today let my marriage be a clear example and message to the world how much You love Your Church. Use my softened heart toward my mate as an avenue to draw people to the gospel. Let our heart connection in marriage make it easier for our children to come to a lifelong faith in You. Finally, may our home be a small foretaste of the joys of heaven. I ask this in Your Name, Lord Jesus, the One who is soon returning for us, Your bride. Amen.

Questions for You and Your Spouse to Discuss

1. Why does the example of a loving and committed marriage have such an impact on others? What will people say was the legacy of your marriage?

2. Which of the nine reasons for keeping a soft heart impresses you most? Which of the negative consequences of a hard heart do you wish most to avoid?

3. Why does it matter that your marriage comes with an expiration date? What steps can you each take today to redeem the days you have left together?

Is a Softened Heart Enough?

WHILE TWO SOFTENED HEARTS can produce The Marriage Miracle, there is always more to experience in our marriages. That's why there's wisdom in pursuing further study and training, in order to build a strong and loving marriage. Now that you have the foundation in place, it becomes only a matter of when, not if, you will enjoy the loving and intimate marriage you desire.

You will still need to give marriage your best effort each day. The more faithful the two of you are in prayer, the more you listen to godly counsel, the more you seek the Holy Spirit's daily guidance, and the more you trust the Word of God, the more your hearts will change.

You will still have to face and overcome obstacles and setbacks. But take heart (we love that phrase), regardless of the pain or disappointments you experience along the way, you have a constant and faithful Friend you can turn to (Hebrews 4:15-16).

Remember, all of heaven desires that your marriage succeed. Listen for God's voice each day, and as you hear it—soften your hearts.

We leave you with a blessing:

To him who is able to keep you from falling and to present you before his glorious presence without fault and with great joy—to the only God our Savior be glory, majesty, power and authority, through Jesus Christ our Lord, before all ages, now and forevermore! Amen (Jude 24-25).

May your hearts be softened for a lifetime.

Appendix I

My Spouse Who Has Hurt Me

Release	Pay
Define each way your spouse has hurt you in the past.	Describe the emotional pain you feel because of the hurt.
1.	
2.	
3.	
4.	
5.	
6.	
7.	
8.	
9.	
10.	

"Lord, I choose to forgive _____ for _____
                                    (name)   (specific hurt)

causing me to feel _____. I am willing to pay for the
                                (emotional pain)

emotional pain and consequences that _____ has caused me. I ask
                                                      (name)

You, Lord Jesus, to take back the ground I gave to the enemy through my bitterness and I yield that ground to Your control."

Appendix 2

Family Members Who Have Hurt Me

List each family member who has hurt you in the past.	**Release** How did they hurt you? (List issues)	**Pay** Describe the emotional pain caused by the hurt.
Father		
Mother		
Stepparents		
Siblings		
Others		

"Lord, I choose to forgive _____ for _____
(name)   (specific hurt)

causing me to feel _____. I am willing to pay for the
(emotional pain)

emotional pain and consequences that _____ has caused me. I ask
(name)

You, Lord Jesus, to take back the ground I gave to the enemy through my bitterness and I yield that ground to Your control."

Appendix 3

People Who Have Hurt Me

List each person who has hurt you in the past.	**Release** How did they hurt you? (List issues)	**Pay** Describe the emotional pain caused by the hurt.
Friends		
Teachers, students, classroom experiences		
Employer, employee		
Believers, church situations, pastor, leader, etc.		
God (List the ways you think God has hurt you.)		
Myself (List each area for which you cannot forgive yourself.)		
Others		

"Lord, I choose to forgive _____ for _____
                                    (name)   (specific hurt)

causing me to feel _____. I am willing to pay for the
                              (emotional pain)

emotional pain and consequences that _____ has caused me. I ask
                                                    (name)

You, Lord Jesus, to take back the ground I gave to the enemy through my bitter-

ness and I yield that ground to Your control."

Appendix 4

Emotional Pain Words

Abandoned
Accused
Afraid
All my fault
Alone
Always wrong
Angry
Annihilated
Anxious
Apathetic
Ashamed
Avoided
Awkward
Babied
Bad
Belittled
Betrayed
Bewildered
Bitter
Blamed
Can't do anything right
Can't trust anyone
Cheap
Cheated
Coerced
Condemned
Confused
Conspired against
Controlled
Cornered
Crushed
Cursed
Cut off
Deceived
Defeated
Defenseless
Defrauded
Degraded
Depressed
Deprived
Deserted
Desires rejected
Despair
Despised
Despondent

Destroyed
Detested
Devalued
Didn't belong
Didn't measure up
Dirty
Disappointed
Discarded
Discounted
Discouraged
Disgraced
Dishonored
Disregarded
Disrespected
Dominated
Embarrassed
Empty
Excluded
Exhausted
Exploited
Exposed
Failure
Fear, fearful
Foolish
Forced
Forsaken
Friendless
Frightened
Frustrated
Good for nothing
Guilty
Hated
Hate myself
Helpless
Hopeless
Humiliated
Hurt
Hysterical
Ignored
Impure
Inadequate
Incompetent
Indecent
Inferior
Inhibited
Insecure

Insensitive to my needs
Insignificant
Invalidated
Isolated
Knocked down
Judged
Left out
Lied to
Lonely
Lost
Made fun of
Manipulated
Mistreated
Misunderstood
Mocked
Molested
Neglected
No good
No support
No way out
Not being affirmed
Not cared for
Not cherished
Not deserving to live
Not listened to
Not measure up
Not valued
Opinions not valued
Overwhelmed
Paralyzed
Powerless
Pressured
Pressure to perform
Publicly shamed
Put down
Rejected
Repulsed
Resentful
Revenge
Ridiculed
Ruined
Sad
Scared
Secluded
Self-disgust

Separated
Shamed
Silenced
Stepped on
Shattered
Stressed
Stupid
Suicidal
Taken advantage of
Terrified
Threatened
Torn apart
Trapped
Trashed
Tricked
Ugly
Unable to speak
Unaccepted
Uncaring
Uncared for
Unchosen
Unclean
Undesirable
Unfairly judged
Unfairly treated
Unfit
Unimportant
Unheard
Unloved
Unlovable
Unnecessary
Unneeded
Unnoticed
Unprotected
Unresponsive
Unsafe
Unwanted
Useless
Valueless
Violated
Vulnerable
Walked on
Wasted
Weak
Worthless
Wounded

Appendix 5

A Personal Heart Examination

Section A

Make two copies of the Personal Heart Exam, one for each of you. Circle any of the following statements that are true about you or the home you grew up in. If the statement concerns you or one of your parents, circle that number if the statement is true some or most of the time. Otherwise, leave the number uncircled. Answer the questions as you would during the worst period of your life, whether that is now or in the past. Instructions for the self-scoring key are found at the end of the exam.

1. I grew up often feeling I was all on my own.
2. I was raised by parents who were too busy to notice me.
3. I was often upset or frightened by my father or mother's temper.
4. I remember being sexually abused by someone when I was growing up.
5. My father or mother could simply shut down their emotions and feel nothing.
6. I was severely criticized for not measuring up to my father or mother's standards.
7. I grew up in an environment where people rarely forgave each other.
8. My father or mother always had to have the last word in any conversation.
9. When one of my parents got depressed, they would ignore or neglect the rest of us.
10. My mother or father would get upset every time someone told them what to do.

11. I discovered pornography in our house.

12. I was taught that a career or earning money is the true measure of success.

13. I felt I was never good enough no matter how hard I tried.

14. When I was hurting, no one reached out to comfort me.

15. I was sometimes spanked too hard or slapped in anger.

16. My dad or mother could easily get emotionally upset.

17. I always got the feeling I was a disappointment to my parents.

18. When I was young I was left alone for hours to take care of myself.

19. It seemed like having money was the one thing that made my parents happy.

20. My father would watch movies with explicit sexual scenes.

21. I grew up being taught to distrust those in authority.

22. One of my parents would go to a room and not come out if they were sad or upset.

23. One of my parents was overly controlling of others.

24. Old hurts and wounds were often rehearsed at our dinner table.

25. Our family was happy when we had money; we were miserable when we were broke.

26. One of my parents had an affair while I was growing up.

27. One of my parents wanted nothing to do with God.

28. I was afraid of making a mistake because of the rejection I would experience.

29. One parent would just walk away if the other parent started to argue with them.

30. I was sometimes slapped or hit with a fist as a form of discipline.

31. I had to emotionally prop up one of my parents when they were sad or depressed.

32. My father or mother would get very upset if they did not get their way.

33. I rarely heard the words, "I forgive you," growing up.

34. One of my parents used profanity and swore often.

35. My parents would make promises to me, and then just forget about them.

36. My father or mother left our home for good when I was young.

37. I sometimes feel I'm going to end up all alone.

38. I could just disappear and no one would care.

39. I often find myself swearing under my breath.

40. The memories of abuse in my home are just too painful to talk about.

41. When someone mistreats me, I can simply disconnect and not feel anything.

42. I have to do everything just right to feel good about myself.

43. I think people should earn my forgiveness if they've hurt me.

44. I have to feel in charge at all times to feel comfortable.

45. I can't focus on the needs of others when I'm really sad.

46. I really don't like having a boss I have to report to; I'd rather work for myself.

47. I spend a good deal of time each day thinking about sexual fantasies.

48. I'll put in long hours overtime at work if I can gain recognition for it.

49. I'm depressed when other people are able to buy nice things I can't afford.

50. I enjoy reading romance novels or watching movies that are steamy.

51. I resent people telling me what to do.

52. I can think only about my own problem(s) until they are resolved.

53. I enjoy telling others what to do; it's the only way to get something done.

54. People who mistreat me should pay the price.

55. Most people are too lazy to do things right; they do just enough to get by.

56. I have no recollection of long periods of my life.

57. Someone used sex to hurt me when I was younger.

58. I often am in trouble for losing my temper.

59. I have to take care of myself; no one else will.

60. I fear people that I love will one day leave me.

61. I find it hard to sympathize with people who are hurting.

62. I try to help people by pointing out their weaknesses or shortcomings.

63. I feel like I'm damaged goods because of the way I was abused.

64. I often regret things I've said in an argument.

65. I frequently forget important things such as anniversaries or birthdays.

66. I worry that someday I will be left for someone else.

67. Making a good living is my number one goal in life.

68. I have a secret sexual fantasy life no one knows anything about.

69. I don't like anyone telling me what to do.

70. I forget about the needs of others when I'm depressed.

71. I've been told I come on too strong with other people.

72. I've been told I have a hard time forgiving others.

73. I've been told I'm too married to my work.

74. I've been told I overreact whenever they ask me to do something.

75. I've been told I tend to dominate others.

76. I've been told I'm too much of a perfectionist.

77. I've been told I don't know how to enjoy life.

78. I've been told I just fall apart when anyone criticizes me.

79. I've been told I need to deal with my frequent sexual thoughts about others.

80. I've been told I just check out of a conversation when it gets intense.

81. I've been told I have trouble asking for forgiveness.

82. I've been told others worry about how often I get depressed.

83. I've been told I have a problem with my temper.

84. I've been told I worry too much about being left all alone in life.

Section B

Please circle the number if the statement is true of your personal thoughts or behavior some or most of the time. If it is not true of your personal thoughts or behavior some or most of the time, leave it uncircled. Again, answer these questions from the perspective of the worst time of your life, whether that is recently or in the past. Instructions for the self-scoring key are found at the end of the exam.

1. I struggle with wicked or evil thoughts toward others.

2. I find myself attracted to movies that include sexual immorality.

3. I take things from others but don't return them.

4. I sometimes wish a person who hurt me were dead.

5. I look at other people with lustful thoughts.

6. I find myself always wanting to have more than what I already own.

7. I can carry a deep grudge toward some people.

8. I will tell a small lie to avoid getting into trouble.

9. I sometimes laugh at dirty jokes.

10. I am often jealous of someone else's looks or accomplishments.

11. I like to think I know better than most people.

12. I will say bad things about other people behind their back.

13. I have made several foolish decisions I later regretted.

14. I disregard the warnings of others if I believe I know better.

15. I like to be the one person that's noticed in a room.

16. I say biting things about other people.

17. I'm sad or upset when other people get recognized and I don't.

18. I enjoy seeing sexually suggestive or illicit scenes in a movie.

19. I sometimes lie when it's just as easy to tell the truth.

20. I hope something bad happens to my enemies.

21. No matter how much money I have, I always seem to want more.

22. I flirt with someone else's spouse now and then.

23. I get so mad at others that I could hurt them.

24. I sometimes cheat a little on income taxes.

25. I was involved in premarital sexual experiences.

26. I sometimes imagine myself doing things that I know are wrong.

27. I struggle with feelings of hatred toward someone.

28. I take things home from the office and don't bring them back.

29. I enjoy making eye contact with an attractive person even if they're married.

30. I really struggle with resentment.

31. I find obscene jokes or stories amusing.

32. Occasionally I will spread damaging information about other people.

33. I don't like consulting with others before I make a big decision.

34. I dwell on sexual experiences I had before I was married.

35. I have to admit there are some people I almost hate.

36. I find myself attracted to owning expensive or nice things.

37. I put on appearances to get people to think what I want them to think.

38. I am upset when someone close to me gets something I really wanted.

39. I associate with people who make me look good.

40. I sometimes have evil thoughts about other people.

41. I will watch a sexually explicit program when no one is looking.

42. I take things from others and don't tell them.

43. I can get so upset with someone that I wish they were dead and gone.

44. I find myself thinking about other potential lovers during sexual intimacy.

45. I am willing to put others in second place if I can get ahead in my finances.

46. I have some feelings of ill will toward others.

47. I sometimes tell white lies.

48. In my mind I bring sensual images from the Internet into my bedroom.

49. I am jealous of others in certain areas.

50. I will reveal confidential or embarrassing things about another person in a conversation.

51. I can handle life on my own.

52. I like taking risky chances with my money even if others warn me.

53. I have deep grievances I've never shared with anyone.

54. Buying something I want makes me happy, but I soon want something else.

55. I think a lot about my former boyfriend or girlfriend even though I'm married.

56. I can't help hating certain people.

57. I take things home from work and don't return them.

58. I like to give a second glance to a sexy person who passes by.

59. I know some of my thoughts are wicked, but I like them anyway.

60. I am a thrill-seeker who likes taking foolish chances.

61. I believe that I'm usually right and other people are usually wrong.

62. I will sometimes say things that could destroy someone else's reputation.

63. I am jealous of other people.

64. I will tell a dirty joke now and then.

65. I often exaggerate to make things sound better than they are.

66. I spend a great deal of time daydreaming about sexual fantasies.

67. I take things without asking.

68. I dwell on how much people I dislike should suffer for their sins.

69. I can hate another person who mistreats me.

70. I find myself looking at people, even if they are married, and wishing we were in a romantic relationship.

71. I can use spiteful words about others.

72. I make quick and impulsive decisions.

73. I like to read all the details about celebrities or politicians who get caught in a sexual scandal.

74. I will punish others with the silent treatment.

75. I push myself to earn more this year than I did last year.

76. I leave people with a false impression of what I'm thinking.

77. I wish I could live the life of someone else rather than my own.

78. I'm wiser than most people I know.

Personal Heart Examination Scoring Key

Using the answer sheets from the Personal Heart Examination, Section A, circle each number you circled in the exam. Then count the number of times you circled a number on each line and put the total at the end of that line under Score.

Section A: The Types of a Hardened Heart								Score
Abandoned Heart	1	14	35	37	60	66	84	_____
Rejected Heart	2	13	33	38	59	65	78	_____
Angry Heart	3	16	34	39	58	64	83	_____
Defiled Heart	4	15	30	40	57	63	77	_____
Detached Heart	5	18	29	41	56	61	80	_____
Judgmental Heart	6	17	28	42	55	62	76	_____
Bitter Heart	7	24	36	43	54	72	81	_____
Controlling Heart	8	23	32	44	53	71	75	_____
Proud Heart	9	22	31	45	52	70	82	_____
Rebellious Heart	10	21	27	46	51	69	74	_____
Immoral Heart	11	20	26	47	50	68	79	_____
Temporal Heart	12	19	25	48	49	67	73	_____

Taking the Next Steps

Now that you've completed the questions in Section A and totaled the score for each type of hardened heart, you should look for the scores that are the highest in number. A score of 0 means you likely do not struggle with this type of hardened heart. A score of 1 or 2 indicates it may be a slight problem, a score of 3 to 5 suggests this is an issue in your life, and a score of 6 or 7 indicates a serious heart issue in this area. You may find you have one or more types of hardened heart in your life.

Take your list and, starting with the highest score, pray through each hardened heart in the following way:

Dear Lord Jesus, I confess that I struggle with a (name the type of hardened heart) that is the result of my painful experiences and sinful choices. I ask Your forgiveness for my hardened heart and choose to renounce a (name the type of hardened heart). I ask You to remove it from my life and in its place to give me a softened heart.

I claim the Bible's promise of Ezekiel 36:26, "I will give you a new heart and put a new spirit in you; I will remove from you your heart of stone and give you a heart of flesh." Thank You, Jesus, that the finished work of the cross has made me a new creation, that the old (name the type of hardened heart) is now gone and the new has come. Keep my new heart soft toward You and others each and every day. In Your Name I pray, amen.

PERSONAL HEART EXAMINATION SCORING KEY

Using the answer sheets from the Personal Heart Examination, Section B, circle each number you circled in the exam. Then count the number of times you circled a number on each line and put the total at the end of that line under Score.

Section B

The Types of Spiritual Issues of a Hardened Heart							Score
Evil Thoughts	1	26	27	40	59	68	_____
Sexual Immorality	2	25	34	41	58	66	_____
Theft	3	24	28	42	57	67	_____
Murder	4	23	30	43	56	69	_____
Adultery	5	22	29	44	55	70	_____
Greed	6	21	36	45	54	75	_____
Malice	7	20	35	46	53	74	_____
Deceit	8	19	37	47	65	76	_____

Lewdness	9	18	31	48	64	73	_____
Envy	10	17	38	49	63	77	_____
Arrogance	11	15	39	51	61	78	_____
Slander	12	16	32	50	62	71	_____
Folly (Foolishness)	13	14	33	52	60	72	_____

Taking the Next Steps

Now that you've completed the questions in Section B and totaled the score for each type of spiritual issue from a hardened heart, look for the scores that are the highest in number. A score of 0 means you likely do not struggle with this type of spiritual issue. A score of 1 or 2 indicates it may be a slight problem, a score of 3 to 5 suggests it is a spiritual issue to address in your life, and a score of 6 or 7 indicates a serious spiritual issue. You may find that you have one or more spiritual issues in your life.

Take your list of spiritual issues and, starting with the highest score, pray through each locked heart in the following way:

> *Dear Lord Jesus, I confess that I struggle with (name the type of spiritual issue) that is the result of my painful experiences and sinful choices. I ask Your forgiveness for allowing this spiritual issue to harden my heart. I ask You to forgive this sin and remove it from my life and in its place to give me a softened heart.*
>
> *I claim the Bible's promise of 1 John 1:7-9, "But if we walk in the light, as he is in the light, we have fellowship with one another, and the blood of Jesus, his Son, purifies us from all sin...If we confess our sins, he is faithful and just and will forgive us our sins and purify us from all unrighteousness."*
>
> *Thank You, Jesus, that through the finished work of the cross, I can find complete forgiveness and freedom from (name the type of spiritual issue). Keep my heart softened toward You and others each and every day. In Your Name I pray, amen.*

Appendix 6

Ask Questions Directed to Their Heart

To understand if they have ever felt loved:

> Have you ever felt loved? If so by whom?
>
> Do you ever feel lonely?
>
> Have you ever had someone care for your emotional needs?
>
> Who did you give your heart to?
>
> Who loved you more than anyone else?
>
> Did you ever give your heart to your dad? mom?
>
> Did your parents ever damage your heart so you pulled it away?
>
> Have you ever given your heart to your spouse? When?
>
> Who has kept you from giving your heart to your spouse?

To understand where their heart is:

> Where is your heart?
>
> Where did you hide your heart when you were hurt in the past?
>
> Who have you fully given your heart to?
>
> Who have you totally trusted to love you?
>
> Have you ever given your heart to me? When? How long?
>
> Do I have your complete heart or have you given it to someone else?

To understand if they have withdrawn their heart because of being hurt:

> Were you ever damaged so severely that you said, "I'll never let anyone do that to me again?"
>
> Has something happened that caused so much pain that you have not been able to open your heart since?

Have you found yourself removing your heart so another person can't hurt you again?

What kind of wall have you built to protect yourself from pain others have caused?

To understand the pain of their past/how they were damaged:

Does another person's anger cause you to struggle inside?

Do you struggle with others' expectations of you?

Have you ever felt rejected? By whom?

Have you ever been made fun of?

Do you react when dominated?

Were you ever affirmed as a child? Praised? Admired? Encouraged?

Were you ever taken advantage of by another person?

Have you ever been crushed by someone who has hurt you?

To understand their emotional needs:

Do you ever cry inside because you feel lonely? How often? When do you cry?

Do you feel valued by me?

What emotional needs do you have? How can I meet them?

Do I take time to listen to the needs of your heart?

Do you ever feel left out?

Am I critical of you?

To understand who they will open their heart to:

Who is a safe person that you would share everything with?

What type of person would you not share anything of your heart with?

© 2007 John Regier. Caring for the Heart Ministries. Used by permission.

Notes

1. Used by permission from John Regier, Caring for the Heart Ministries, 2008.

2. John Regier, *Rekindling Marital Intimacy* (Colorado Springs: Biblical Concepts in Counseling, 1999).

3. Emerson Eggerichs, *Love and Respect* (Nashville: Thomas Nelson Publishers, 2004).

4. William Strom, *Communicating Humility in Marriage: A Qualitative Study,* p. 21 (www.allacademic.com//meta/p_mla_apa_research_citation/1/8/6/4/4/pages186447/p186447-21.php).

5. For further explanation of the Holy Spirit's role in our lives, see J. I. Packer, *Keep in Step with the Spirit* (Grand Rapids, MI: Baker Books, 2005) and Bill Bright, *Have You Made the Wonderful Discovery of the Spirit-Filled Life?* (Peachtree City, GA: New Life Resources, 1990).

6. See www.heritage.org/research/family/.

7. See www.quotedb.com/quotes/1905.

8. See www.facebook.com/topic.php?uid=8415951356&topic=10487.

About the Authors

Bob and Cheryl Moeller are the cofounders of For Better, For Worse, For Keeps Ministries, a nonprofit ministry dedicated to helping couples connect their hearts for a lifetime. Bob conducts conferences throughout the year for married couples and for singles (the conferences are also available on CD). For more information on hosting or attending a conference, or to order the CDs, go to www.boband cherylmoeller.com.

Bob and Cheryl have authored several other books on marriage including, *For Better, For Worse, For Keeps: God's Gift of Hope for Every Marriage* and *Marriage Minutes: 365 Inspirational Readings to Share with your Spouse*. They also have a book for singles titled *The Road to "I Do."*

Bob is the weekly on-air television host of a live call-in program, *Marriage—For Better, For Worse*. The program is carried across the nation on the Total Living Network (www.tln.com) and the Sky Angel IPTV. Bob also appears as a frequent guest on radio call-in programs on both the Moody Broadcasting Network and the Faith Radio Network. He also has a sixty-second daily devotional called "The Marriage Minute" that airs on TLN television and various radio stations across the country.

Cheryl, a homemaker and mom, uses her over-the-countertop humor to show you the laughter in the everydayness of life through her speaking, syndicated column, books, and blog (www.momlaughs.blogspot.com). Her book, *Keep Courting: 100 Ways to Keep Courting After Marriage,* is available on her website. If you're interested in bringing Cheryl's unique brand of comedy and spiritual warmth to your women's group, church, or event, contact her at: office@bobandcherylmoeller.com.

Bob holds a Doctor of Ministry degree and Cheryl a Master of Arts in Religion, and they have been married thirty years. They are the proud parents of six children, one son-in-law, and have three dogs with rather large appetites.

Our Mission: To help disciple married couples into a growing and thriving relationship with God and each other so that they might in turn effectively display the love of God to their neighbors and around the world.

MarriageVine is passionate about growing healthy marriages. We minister to thousands every day through our resources, events, counseling, and online content. Visit us at www.MarriageVine.com.